# A PASSION FOR MUSHROOMS

*Antonio Carluccio*

# A PASSION FOR
# MUSHROOMS

**PAVILION**

I dedicate this book to my mother and to my wife Priscilla.

This edition published in 1990.
First published in Great Britain in 1989 by
PAVILION BOOKS LIMITED
196 Shaftesbury Avenue, London WC2H 8JL


Text copyright © Antonio Carluccio 1989
Illustrations copyright © Flo Bayley 1989
Food photography by Andrew Whittuck © Pavilion Books 1989
Mushroom photography copyright © Roger Phillips 1981
In situ photography copyright © David Thomas 1989

Designed by Bernard Higton

A CIP catalogue record for this book is available from
the British Library.

ISBN 1-85145-113-7 (Hbk)
ISBN 1-85145-542-6 (Pbk)

Filmset by Tradespools Ltd., Frome
Colour separation by C.L.G., Verona, Italy
Printed and bound by Arnoldo Mondadori Ltd., Verona, Italy

10 9 8 7 6 5 4 3

**The author and publishers believe the information
contained in this book to be correct and
accurate at the time of going to press. Cooking and
eating wrongly identified mushrooms can be fatal.
If ever in doubt, don't. Neither the author nor the
publishers can accept any legal responsibility
or liability for any errors, omissions or mistaken
identification of fungus species that may be made.**

# CONTENTS

# INTRODUCTION

**E**verything about wild mushrooms is a pleasure to me.

There is the early-morning atmosphere of woods and hills, heavy with expectation; and even on those days when you find nothing, the wonderful damp autumn wood-smells seem *almost* worth the bleary-eyed stumble from bed.

There is the mystery of the secret places where you *know* there should be a cep or a chanterelle – but mushrooms are unpredictable, always surprising or challenging, presenting some unfathomable link with nature in our otherwise routine and sophisticated lives. With one or two exceptions, mushrooms defy science's attempts to domesticate them: they retain an element of mystery and wildness, you have to go out and find them – and the wild ones you find always taste infinitely better.

There is all the excitement of the hunt. I think most of us have a very primitive hunting instinct, but the mushroom hunt is an innocent one because (within reason) gathering these fungus fruit-bodies causes no harm, and helps distribute their spores.

There is the very satisfying simplicity of the tools of the trade – a good old traditional woven basket or trug to transport the mushrooms unharmed (no plastic bags here) and a knife – one of a collection from all over the world, each one with a story to tell...

I remember so vividly, as a child in Italy, my pride and sense of achievement at returning home with a basketful of mushrooms. My spoils would be spread out on the kitchen table, sorted and praised, and then turned by my mother into all sorts of delightful tastes. I

was so proud at making a contribution to the family's eating. Mushroom hunting was a serious autumnal routine – albeit a pleasurable one: part of the everyday task of feeding the family and preserving for the winter ahead. For some people it was a livelihood.

Mushroom hunting was a habit I took with me when I went to live first in Austria and then in Germany, where I combed the woods around Hamburg with my faithful dog Jan – and with considerable numbers of like-minded rivals. Imagine my disorientation when I brought my finely tuned hunting instincts to Britain and found not only that the hills were alive with mounds of mushrooms – but that I was virtually alone in pursuit of them: where was the cutthroat competition of the European autumn scene? Occasionally I met a fellow enthusiast, but often I had the field to myself: I did not even have to get up at daybreak to get the mushrooms.

For a time I found myself in something of a quandary. My 'training' led me to want to keep for myself the mushrooms I found and the locations where I found them. On the

other hand, my instincts were for sharing. Somehow the more generous motive won – the pleasure of seeing other people enjoying all aspects of mushrooms as much as I do outweighs the possessive urge. It has become a type of crusade on my part to convince the doubtful and convert the unbelieving. My restaurant has become a sort of mushroom mecca in the autumn. Even in this civilized urban context, the pleasures connected with mushrooms continue to be unpredictable and surprising. Strangers telephone me with news of bountiful crops. People leave basketfuls on my doorstep or send mysterious packages through the post. There is a gentle rivalry between restaurateurs, as between mushroom hunters in the field. I keep making new mycological friends. And I am always learning, always discovering new mushrooms and new ways of eating them.

This book is itself a sort of mushroom, the visible 'fruiting' of my very long-standing enthusiasm. First of all I try to disseminate my ideas on how to prepare, cook and preserve some of my favourite edible mushrooms, and in the seven recipe chapters of this culinary section, to show their great versatility. In the second part of the book I present a field guide to help you identify these, as well as some of the most dangerous species.

I wish you luck with your hunting and success with your cooking – with the warning: whenever in doubt about the identity of a mushroom, *don't* risk eating it!

# —PART 1—
# THE RECIPES

## EATING MUSHROOMS

The best-known mushroom must be *Agaricus bisporus* – the 'champignon', cultivated in France since the time of Louis XIV. Biomycologists all over the world are trying to domesticate more species, but unfortunately few wild mushrooms seem to be amenable to cultivation on a large scale. In recent years *Pleurotus ostreatus* (oyster mushroom) has been cultivated with some success, and it seems that *Armillaria mellea* (honey fungus) is giving up its secrets. In the Far East *Lentinula edodes* (shiitake) and *Volvariella volvacea* (padi straw) mushrooms have been cultivated successfully for many years. Attempts in France and Italy to grow truffles have only partly succeeded, and much of the process is still left to nature. For all the other species one still has to trust to nature and to one's own luck on mushroom-gathering forays, or to the almost equally capricious market forces of price and availability.

Of the five thousand or so wild mushrooms that grow in Europe, 'only' about 1,200 are thought to be edible. There is a fairly general consensus placing some twenty edible species at the very top in terms of quality, safety and availability. About thirty mushrooms are very poisonous and another thirty or so are suspect. This is a rough guide, but it serves to illustrate how few poisonous specimens there are compared to edible ones.

The definition of 'edibility' is, of course, something of a movable feast. A handful of mushrooms are universally acknowledged as gastronomically superb for both flavour and versatility; a lot more are praised or dismissed according to the opinion of the person who is passing judgement. This is partly a question of taste in the most literal sense, partly, perhaps, a cultural matter: in Italy, people will ignore delicious mushrooms in their single-minded quest for porcini, even regarding with suspicion the *Agaricus* species – the field and horse mushrooms that are the *only* ones many British people will eat at all.

Local markets all over Europe sell wild mushrooms in season, gathered by professional collectors whose supply is systematically checked before appearing on the stalls and in the shops. Many European governments appoint specially trained officers to inspect mushrooms before they are sold. In Trento, you can find up to 35

different species of edible mushrooms on the market, and the purchaser can be confident they have all been safely 'vetted'. There is also a minor industry collecting desirable species such as ceps for the busy commercial concerns that dry and preserve wild mushrooms.

Mushroom appreciation is full of contrasts and contradictions: on the one hand, wild mushrooms are often considered peasants' food – eaten by more sophisticated people only to supplement dietary shortages during wartime; on the other, city people in restaurants pay dearly for the privilege of eating this same 'peasant' food, which is gathered for free and transported at considerable expense. In some communities the autumn hunting season involves all the family in gathering sufficient to preserve for the winter, and people go to some lengths to render edible mushrooms that others would consider toxic. And at the other extreme refined palates appreciate the sought-after truffle, perhaps speculating whether this 'black diamond' fulfils its reputed aphrodisiac properties. (No special effects have been scientifically proven: it may be that the very high price of some commodities like truffles and caviare causes excitement akin to sensuality!)

## FOOD VALUE OF MUSHROOMS

Other attributes of mushrooms are easier to measure. Most mushrooms consist of approximately 90 per cent water and contain various important minerals – potassium salts, phosphates, niacin, plus varying quantities of vitamins B1, B2, C and D. In nutritional terms, the key qualities of a mushroom are the low calorie content (only 35 per 100g), the low fat (1–2 per cent) and the protein content (3–9 per cent). But it is texture and flavour (and in certain cases a unique aromatic quality) that make mushrooms generally so indispensable in cooking.

The most sensible way to approach eating wild mushrooms is with caution. This applies not only to the need to identify them accurately; even those acknowledged to be edible can cause gastric upsets in individuals. The micro-structure of mushrooms makes them less digestible than many other plants and the stomach juices take longer to break them down. Never over-indulge with mushroom eating: it is best to limit portions to 100–150g/4–6oz. Even good edible mushrooms can become indigestible if not treated or prepared properly. The rule is to eat them as fresh as possible and to choose only the best specimens. Deterioration can take place in perfectly good mushrooms during unsuitable storage (and that includes transport from the gathering site to the kitchen in a plastic bag), producing damaging toxins.

Some mushrooms are inedible unless cooked or blanched before cooking: the Field Guide indicates any such necessary preparations under the individual species.

## DEALING WITH YOUR MUSHROOM HARVEST

A common autumn spectacle in Italy is that of a group of people sitting around a table piled high with mushrooms, sorting and cleaning them, and deciding what is to be done with them. Mushrooms don't improve once they have been gathered, and even if you have picked only a few handfuls, you too should perform this ritual as soon as you get home to avoid the disappointment of finding that your prizes have gone soggy overnight, or that the maggots have had a feast in your stead. If you have had a good harvest, call all hands on deck to help.

The ritual involves different tasks. There is the vital precaution of having someone knowledgeable check the identity and edibility of each specimen. There is the practical quality-control aspect of cleaning, inspecting and sorting into size and type. There is the creative challenge of assessing the best way to make the most of them – deciding what delicious thing to do with each one. Sometimes a special find calls out for a particular accompaniment, and you rush out to buy a fish or a fowl to make a special meal. Sometimes a tiny amount of something special needs ekeing out. Sometimes, perhaps most often, you just have a miscellaneous assortment, which if not gourmet material is at least versatile. Sometimes what you have will all be consumed straight away; sometimes there's enough to sort out some for preserving – and by what method?

Suppose you have come back from the woods with a small basketful of mixed fungi. If they are extremely fresh and tender you might make a Fritto misto or capture their flavour in Gruzzoletti. However, if they look a bit tired then soups, stews, casseroles or beignets are natural resting places. For quite elderly specimens, drying is the best bet. You might have found a nice big 'cauliflower' of *Sparassis crispa* or a cluster of *Armillaria mellea* (honey fungus): after you have put aside enough for a sauce to accompany a lovely plate of pasta and perhaps cooked some for a stew, cook the rest in vinegar to preserve as antipasto – to eat yourself or put in little jars and give away.

Suppose your basket contains a substantial number of a single species – *Boletus edulis* if you are very lucky. Sort them out by size, putting them into separate piles according to whether they are small and firm (incidentally, the most expensive to buy), medium, big-and-young or big-but-old. Do your cleaning and maggot-excising. Once you can see how much good mushroom material you have, you can survey the options for eating them:

small ones in prime condition – slice raw in salads

small and medium: sauté for immediate use or for deep freezing; or deep-freeze, sliced or whole; or slice and preserve in oil

big and young (pores still creamy-coloured): grill whole, or slice and use as above

big but elderly: slice for drying, or for immediate cooking

bits and pieces, old and young: dry for powdering, or cook into extract

Even with one solitary mushroom (though preferably a biggish one) you can make a dish. If you have a single cep, slice it thinly, fry in butter in a small pan, add some scrambled egg, season with salt and pepper and there you are – something special.

## COOKING METHODS

Although my recipe instructions specify *how* to cook the mushroom ingredients in all cases, I include these notes to help explain *why*, as well as to offer a summary of processes for you to draw on to develop your own recipes.

**Frying** in oil, or butter, or a mixture of both, in a pan: when you sauté mushrooms briefly in very hot fat, add seasoning at the end – especially garlic, which should on no account be allowed to brown, and salt, which makes the mushrooms exude water and alters taste. I find a mixture helps prevent the butter turning brown, or I use oil first and add butter at a later stage to give sauces a nice taste and shiny, creamy look. The purpose of this method is to cook the outside so it is nice and crispy, sealing in the flavour, and it is a good thing to do straight away, since it is the first stage of any number of recipes: mushrooms treated like this keep for a few hours or can be frozen.

**Sautéing** over low heat – the equivalent of stewing – is good for dealing with a combination of fresh and dry mushrooms. Flavour is exuded with the juices, making a delicious sauce.

**Grilling** is good for substantial mushrooms – big caps of cep, Caesar's mushroom, parasol, *Agaricus* species, slices of giant puffball; also chunks of ready-blanched cauliflower mushroom.

**Blanching** is sometimes a useful precaution for preserving young ink caps in their closed state, for example, but is sometimes a necessary measure to remove toxins present in raw mushrooms.

**Deep-frying** is a favourite method of mine: dip mushrooms in beaten egg and then in breadcrumbs and deep-fry – this seals in flavour and gives an appetizing crispy texture to the outside.

**Microwaving** is not recommended for cooking mushrooms, but is useful for reheating dishes – once only.

## THE RECIPES

I have based the recipe chapters roughly according to how we eat in Italy. Antipasti are hors d'oeuvre, preceding other courses and specifically designed to stimulate the appetite for what is to follow. 'Il primo' is strictly the first course – in the past it was the 'filler' or bulk food for poor families. Today although still based on pasta or rice, primi dishes are usually offered in smaller quantities because followed by other food. Next in the Italian meal comes 'Il secondo', which I have split into fish on the one hand and meat and game on the other, but I have also included an anomalous chapter of 'Piatti di mezzo' – odd snacks or dishes to eat at any time. The Italian meal might end with a dessert to finish in 'Bellezza', as they say, a good meal, and I have added a chapter on preserving to take you into the future.

Quantities are given in metric, imperial and American cup measures, and you are advised to choose one system or another and use it consistently to keep proportions right in any given recipe.

I hope you enjoy cooking my recipes. You may discover you need more salt here and more pepper there; you may decide to make more radical adaptations and improvements; or you may use my ideas as a starting point for new culinary experiments. I leave it to your imagination – reiterating my warning *not* to experiment with any mushrooms you are not sure about. *Buon appetito!*

# ANTIPASTI

**T**he word *antipasto* is derived from ante (meaning before) and pasto (meaning meal). Since the purpose of an antipasto is to tease the appetite before a meal and there are two or three courses to follow, it is never served in large amounts.

Antipasti vary considerably from region to region in Italy, from a few slices of home-made salami or some anchovies in green sauce to pickled artichokes, gherkins and aubergines – and, above all, pickled porcini, the speciality of northern Italy, where an antipasto without pickled mushrooms is no antipasto at all. Special industries preserve tiny porcini in olive oil and present them artistically in large jars. You can buy them in the best Italian delicatessens all over the world. They are expensive even in Italy, and consequently are served in small portions just to sample the taste and whet the appetite.

Mushroom-lovers preserve their own delicacies throughout the season and keep them religiously in the larder until some special occasion when friends or relatives share the delight of eating them and recalling memories of the hunts that took place during the long summer days. (And with the recipes for preserving mushrooms in my final chapter, you too can join that happy band.)

In season, the great variety of freshly picked wild mushrooms are cooked or prepared in many different ways and served both as antipasti and as snacks suitable for any occasion. Perhaps one of the nicest things is to come home hungry and discover some left-over antipasti in the fridge – what a feast!

## FANTASY IN BLACK AND WHITE

### Fantasia in bianco e nero

The idea for this recipe came to me when the famous chef Anton Mosimann, then of the Dorchester Hotel, was giving an important dinner for the launch of a particular new book. The menus had already been printed, but by the afternoon preceding the dinner he still didn't have any white truffles to complete the recipes included in the menu. I was the only restaurateur in London at the time to possess a kilo of fresh white truffles, so I gave him a good proportion of them so that he could prepare the dishes he had planned. I wasn't able to be there myself, but I heard later that the event was a complete success.

This, then, is my version of the Fantasy in Black and White. Assuming you are able to find enough truffles, I can tell you that this dish is a dream – in fact, a fantasy.

*Serves 4*

| |
|---|
| 2 × *Tuber magnatum* (white Alba truffles) weighing about 20g/¾oz each |
| 2 × *Tuber melanosporum* (black truffles) weighing about 10g/scant ½oz each |
| 2 tbsp Armagnac |
| 50g/2oz/4 tbsp butter |
| salt and pepper to taste |
| 4 slices white bread for toasting |
| parsley to garnish |

Cut the truffles into slices about 2.5mm/¹⁄₁₀in thick. Place them in a bowl with the Armagnac and let them marinate for 1 hour. Melt the butter in a pan over a moderate heat but don't let it brown. Add the truffles and the Armagnac, add salt and pepper to taste, cover and allow to simmer for 4–5 minutes. Meanwhile, make the toast. Arrange alternate slices of black and white truffle in a circle on each piece of toast. Decorate with a small sprig of parsley and serve hot.

## BEEF WITH TRUFFLES ALBA-STYLE

### Carne all'albese

Once my wife and I were in the Monferrato region of Italy towards the end of September. We were exploring the area where, during the war and for a time afterwards, I grew up. We had reached a little town called Monbaruzzo which is famous for its wonderful amaretti, and feeling hungry, we decided to stop for lunch and asked some locals if they could direct us to the *caffé della stazione*. Not knowing what to expect, we approached the caffé-ristorante with a little apprehension but plenty of enthusiasm.

The *sala per mangiare* was laid out next to the bar where the perennial TV was switched on. A few *operai* (local workers) were having their 'civilized' lunch – in that part of the world it isn't enough for them just to have a few sandwiches. What they had on their plates looked extremely tempting and encouraging. My immediate impression was that behind the scenes there was a good old Italian motherly type at the stove preparing this wonderful food, and my impression proved to be correct.

I could never have imagined that we would be offered Carne all'albese as a starter. This rather sophisticated dish is sometimes confused with Carpaccio, but only the meat base is common to both dishes – to qualify for the name 'all'albese', the white truffle must be included. But this was, after all, the land of the white Alba truffle. What remained after an excellent meal was not only the memory of the wonderful flavours, but also the satisfaction of knowing that at such reasonable prices everyone could afford them. This luxury was all so natural and matter-of-fact there that we were quite stunned.

*Serves 4*

| |
|---|
| 400g/14oz very tender beef such as fillet, cut very thinly |
| juice of 1 lemon |
| 2 tbsp olive oil |
| salt and pepper to taste |
| 1 × 50g/2oz *Tuber magnatum* (white Alba truffle), cleaned |

Beat the slices of beef even thinner, placing them between two plastic sheets to avoid tearing the meat. Arrange the slices on four plates, sprinkle with lemon juice and olive oil and add salt and pepper to taste. Only when the plates are on the dining table do you slice the truffle very thinly over the dish, using a 'mandolino' cutter. Serve with grissini sticks.

FANTASY IN BLACK AND WHITE

## SALAD OF CAESAR'S MUSHROOMS AND CEPS

### Insalata di ovoli e porcini

*Amanita caesarea* and *Boletus edulis* are the mushrooms *par excellence* to eat raw in a salad. The Italians, particularly in the north, are infatuated with both, and you will find them on the menus of all the best restaurants. They are indeed a delicacy, and I urge you to try them as soon as possible. You need small specimens, not only because they will be firm enough to slice very thin, but also because they are much less likely to contain any 'sitting tenants' – my term for maggots.

If by chance you happen to be the fortunate owner of a small white truffle and slice it very thinly over this salad, then you have indeed reached the Nirvana stage of every gourmet's dream. Even if you have to make do with parsley, this salad is delicious.

| *Serves 4* |
| --- |
| 200g/7oz small fresh *Amanita caesarea* (Caesar's mushroom) or *Boletus edulis* (cep), or 150g/5oz of each |
| 4 tbsp good olive oil (but not virgin, as it is too strong) |
| juice of 1 lemon |
| salt and pepper to taste |
| 1 × 20g/¾oz *Tuber magnatum* (white Alba truffle), or 1 tsp chopped parsley |

Clean the mushrooms, using a small knife to scrape away any stubborn dirt and a damp cloth for a final wipe. Slice the mushrooms thinly into a bowl, add the oil, lemon juice and salt and pepper to taste. Mix carefully together. At the last moment, sprinkle with parsley or, using a 'mandolino', grate the truffle over the top. Serve with grissini sticks.

## PIO CESARE'S BREAKFAST

### Uova al tegame Pio Cesare

This recipe describes a typical breakfast for Mr Pio Cesare. This lucky man is a well-known producer of fine Piedmontese wines. One day he came into my restaurant for lunch, and told me mouth-watering stories of the occasions when his workers would go into the woods truffle-hunting for him, and return with magnificent truffles which he would eat for his breakfast.

This recipe is so wonderful that I just had to include it on my menu as an antipasto, with overwhelming success. You could also serve it as part of a main course.

Pio also explained to me that if you place truffles in a container with some eggs for a day or so, the eggs absorb an amazing amount of the scent of the truffles, even through the shells, enhancing the flavour of the dish.

*Serves 4*

| FOR THE BAGNA CAUDA |
| --- |
| 6 large cloves garlic |
| 1 glass milk (or enough to cover the garlic) |
| 10 anchovy fillets |
| 2 tbsp double (heavy) cream |
| YOU WILL ALSO NEED |
| 8 large, fresh free-range eggs |
| 4 tbsp pure olive oil (not virgin) |
| 1 × 50–60g/2oz *Tuber magnatum* (white Alba truffle), cleaned |
| good, fresh, white bread for serving |

First prepare the *bagna cauda*. Put the garlic and the milk into a small saucepan and simmer over a low heat until the garlic is very soft (about 20 minutes). Add the anchovies and stir over heat until the anchovies have dissolved. Remove from the heat and pass through a very fine sieve to separate any remaining fish bones. Stir in the double cream, and the *bagna cauda* is ready.

Make each serving separately: take two eggs, separate the whites from the yolks carefully, without breaking the yolk. Pour 1 tbsp olive oil into a small non-stick frying pan and heat. When the oil is hot, add the two egg whites, and reduce the heat. When this has solidified add a quarter of the *bagna cauda* mixture and then gently add the yolks, which should just become warm and very runny.

Serve on hot plates and just before eating, use a 'mandolino' to shave a quarter of the truffle per person over the top. The very reviving aroma which emanates from this dish is sublime. The fresh white bread is necessary to absorb the yolk and other succulent goodies.

## GRILLED MUSHROOMS

### Funghi alla griglia

Anyone who has been in Italy during the mushroom season must have eaten some of those wonderful grilled cep caps – *cappelle di porcini alla griglia*. The wonderful flavour comes from oil dripping down on to the hot charcoal and the resulting smoke permeating the mushrooms. Grilling is a typical way of preparing the large caps not only of *porcini* but also of *ovoli* (*Amanita caesarea*); less common but also excellent are large caps of *Agaricus arvensis* and *Lepiota procera* and large slices of giant puffball (*Langermannia gigantea*). With the exception, perhaps, of *Leccinum versipelle* which blackens and is not worth while, most mushroom caps are good cooked this way, even large open caps of the cultivated mushrooms. If you cook the side with the gills or pores first, you will retain more juiciness in the flesh.

*Serves 4*

| 1 large (10–15cm/4–6in diameter) mushroom cap per person, cleaned |
| --- |
| garlic olive oil for brushing the mushrooms (or a few tbsp olive oil in which you have steeped 1 peeled clove of garlic for at least 1 hour) |
| 1 tbsp very finely chopped parsley |
| salt |
| freshly ground black pepper |

Preheat the grill. Brush the top surface of the caps with the garlic-flavoured oil mixed with the chopped parsley, and sprinkle on a little salt. Place top side upwards on the grill and cook for about 4–5 minutes, depending on the thickness of the cap. Turn the caps over, pour a little oil into the centre of each, sprinkle again with salt and continue to grill until cooked. Season with freshly ground black pepper. Serve with good fresh bread.

PIO CESARE'S BREAKFAST

## Sautéed Mushrooms

### Funghi saltati in padella

This universal recipe is not only suitable as a small antipasto, but also as a basic recipe to be served as a side dish accompanying any kind of food.

I have tried this method with all the wild mushrooms described in this book, naturally cutting the larger ones into smaller pieces and blanching those that require it. The cultivated champignon, shiitake and oyster mushrooms are also very good. It is perhaps unnecessary for me to point out that the truffle is excluded from this method, and that the best results are obtained with the boletes. If you wish, you can mix all sorts of wild mushrooms together for this dish; however, it is essential to choose only the small, firm specimens.

*Serves 4*

| |
|---|
| 675g/1½ lb wild mushrooms of your choice, cleaned |
| 60g/2oz/4 tbsp butter |
| 4 tbsp good olive oil |
| 1 clove garlic, finely chopped |
| 1 tbsp finely chopped fresh parsley |
| salt and pepper to taste |

Heat the butter and oil in a frying pan; when hot, add the mushrooms and stir-fry over a lively heat for 10 minutes. Some mushrooms may exude a lot of moisture – if they have been collected soon after rain, they almost certainly will. In this case, continue to sauté until the water has evaporated. Add the garlic and sauté further for a couple of minutes; then add the parsley, salt and pepper to taste, and serve straight away.

## MUSHROOM, SPINACH AND BACON SALAD

### Insalata di funghi, spinaci e pancetta

I have tried this recipe using cultivated shiitake mushrooms with excellent results, but a more intense flavour is obtained with wild mushrooms such as *Armillaria mellea*, *Cantharellus cibarius*, *Hydnum repandum*, *Lactarius deliciosus*, *Laetiporus sulphureus*, *Leccinum versipelle*, *Lepiota procera*, *Lepista nuda* or the *Suillus* species. If you use *Boletus badius* and/or *B. edulis* you will find you can omit the bacon, because these distinctive mushrooms do not require that additional flavouring.

The secret lies in the fresh crispness of the raw spinach (which should be the curly Continental type rather than coarse-leaved beet) combining with piping-hot succulent morsels of bacon and mushroom.

| *Serves 4* |
| --- |
| 280g/10oz tender leaves of Continental spinach (cleaned weight) |
| 150g/5oz streaky bacon, cut into fine strips |
| 2 tbsp olive oil |
| 300g/10oz wild mushrooms, cleaned and cut into fine strips |
| FOR THE VINAIGRETTE |
| 4 tbsp olive oil |
| 1 tbsp sweet mustard |
| 1 tbsp vinegar |
| a pinch of sugar |
| salt and pepper to taste |

Wash the spinach thoroughly in cold water, drain and pat dry, taking care not to bruise it: use only the tenderest leaves. Arrange on four plates.

Prepare the vinaigrette by mixing all the ingredients thoroughly.

Fry the bacon strips in the olive oil for 3–4 minutes, stir, then add the strips of mushroom and sauté over a high heat for 3–4 minutes, depending on the tenderness of the mushrooms. Pour a quarter of the vinaigrette over each portion of spinach, divide the fried mixture equally between the plates, and serve straight away.

## SCRAMBLED EGGS WITH TRUFFLE

### Uova strapazzate al tartufo

I never usually have breakfast myself, except on those occasions when I go out early in the morning on a mushroom hunt, when the combination of fatigue and freshly picked mushrooms seems to induce a certain appetite. In America and other places where large breakfasts or brunches are commonplace this dish would be ideal – served, perhaps, with a glass of champagne instead of coffee.

The degree of sophistication achieved by shaving a black or white truffle over simple scrambled eggs is unbelievable. The 'vehicle' of scrambled eggs is versatile enough to use with almost every different type of mushroom. You could replace the truffle in this recipe with freshly picked chanterelles, ceps, *Boletus badius*, small *Coprinus comatus*, horn of plenty – or even field mushrooms, although in these cases the chopped mushrooms would need to be lightly sautéed in some butter before being combined with the eggs.

*Serves 4*

| |
|---|
| 60g/2oz/4 tbsp unsalted butter |
| 8 large, fresh free-range eggs |
| salt and pepper |
| 2 tbsp double (heavy) cream |
| 4 slices white bread, toasted and buttered |
| 1 × 50g/2oz *Tuber magnatum* (white Alba truffle) or *T. melanosporum* (black truffle) cleaned |

Melt the butter in a non-stick frying pan but do not allow to brown. Beat the eggs in a bowl and add salt and pepper to taste. Pour the egg mixture into the frying pan and stir from time to time to loosen any flecks of cooked egg from the bottom of the pan. Continue until you see that all the egg mixture is just starting to solidify. Remove from the heat and stir into the mixture (which should still be slightly runny) the cream. Mix well and serve on the toast. When placed in front of the guests, shave thin slices of truffle over each portion using a 'mandolino' – and *Buon appetito*!

## MY DUCK LIVER PÂTÉ

### Il mio paté di fegato

I call this recipe 'mine', but I must admit that the influence of Santiago Gonzales, chef at my restaurant for the last 16 years and master in the preparation of foie gras, was crucial for the realization of this dish. It has little or nothing to do with that very expensive industrially made stuff you can buy in which a so-called truffle is situated in the centre of the pâté and tastes of nothing. As soon as you can get some truffles, try to make this pâté – it is truly delicious.

*Serves 4*

| |
|---|
| 80g/3oz pork fat, chopped |
| 1 small onion, chopped |
| 4 cloves garlic, chopped |
| 500g/1 lb 2oz cleaned duck livers, coarsely chopped |
| 2 bay leaves |
| 1 sprig rosemary |
| salt and pepper to taste |
| small glass of dry sherry |
| small glass of brandy |
| 60g/2oz/4 tbsp butter |
| 1 × 25g/1oz *Tuber aestivum* or *T. melanosporum* (black truffle), cleaned |
| a little aspic or gelatine for garnish (optional) |

Put the pork fat in a pan, stir-fry for 3–4 minutes, add the onion, and stir-fry until the onion is transparent. Now add the garlic, the chopped liver, the bay leaves and the rosemary, and continue to stir-fry for another 5 minutes over a moderate heat. Add the salt, pepper, brandy and sherry. Let the alcohol evaporate for one minute, add the butter and set aside to cool a little. Remove and discard the bay leaves and the rosemary and if you wish put the rest into a blender just for a few seconds – it should still have some texture. Now place the mixture in a terrine. Press the truffle into the mixture so that it is just under the surface. Put the terrine in a bain marie (a large tray containing 2cm/1in water will do). Place in a preheated oven and cook at a moderate temperature (180°C/350°F/Gas Mark 4) for 1 hour. Take out and allow to cool. Cut into slices, and if you want to decorate it for a cold buffet, you can garnish the slices with some gelatine or aspic, cut into little cubes.

## BLACK TRUFFLE CROSTINI

### Crostini al tartufo nero

Crostini are the most famous hors-d'oeuvre of Tuscany. The principle is to have as a vehicle unsalted Tuscan bread which has been toasted and then spread with different toppings such as quail liver pâté, olive paste, etc. The crostini can be served warm or cold with an aperitif, or can be used to start a meal. This version with black truffles can be very costly indeed, but it can be made more economical if you cut the truffle very thinly and use it just for the flavour. The nearest thing to unsalted Tuscan bread in countries outside Italy is pale, coarse wholemeal bread.

*Serves 4*

| |
|---|
| 1 clove garlic, finely chopped |
| 2 tsp green peppercorns |
| 200g/7oz chicken livers |
| 60g/2oz *Tuber aestivum* or *T. melanosporum* (black truffles) |
| 3 tbsp virgin olive oil |
| 1 tsp brandy |
| juice of ½ lemon |
| salt and pepper to taste |
| 4 large slices of wholemeal bread for toasting |

Place the garlic and the green peppercorns in a mortar and reduce to pulp. Cut the well-trimmed livers and the truffle into small cubes. Heat the olive oil in a frying pan; when hot, fry the livers and truffle. After 5 minutes of moderate stir-frying, add the mixture from the mortar and cook for another 2 minutes. Add the brandy and lemon juice, season with salt and pepper and amalgamate. Toast the wholemeal bread. Spread the mixture evenly on the toast, cut into small pieces and serve straight away.

## MY MUSHROOM SALAD

### La mia insalata di funghi

Whenever I return from a successful mushroom hunt I prepare this tasty dish right away. I use the smallest and firmest specimens of *Boletus edulis* and *B. badius*, since a salad calls for freshly picked mushrooms in peak condition. I deliberately put the two types of mushroom together because of their difference in texture: the slightly softer flesh of *Boletus badius* contrasts with the

more crunchy consistency of the cep, a combination creating a nice sensation on the palate.

*Serves 4*

| |
|---|
| 150g/5oz small fresh *Boletus edulis* (cep), cleaned |
| 150g/5oz small fresh *Boletus badius* (bay bolete), cleaned |
| 4 tbsp garlic olive oil (prepare by steeping 3–4 peeled and slightly crushed garlic cloves in olive oil for 2–3 hours) |
| 1 tbsp lemon juice |
| 1 tbsp dry white wine |
| salt and pepper to taste |
| 1 tbsp finely chopped parsley |

Cut the mushrooms very thinly lengthwise and arrange on a deep porcelain plate. In a separate bowl mix the garlic olive oil, lemon juice, wine and salt and pepper into a sort of emulsion. Sprinkle evenly over the mushroom slices and place in the refrigerator for 1 hour. Before serving, sprinkle with parsley. Eat with grissini.

## ANTIPASTO WITH PRESERVED MUSHROOMS

### Antipasto misto con funghi

Until you are able to preserve your own mushrooms, I suggest that you buy some preserved ones from your local delicatessen. Porcini sott'olio are available almost everywhere; they are not cheap but you need only use three or four per portion, depending on size, and make up the missing quantities with something else: all the ingredients listed below are easily available from a good Italian delicatessen. You can, however, start to practise preserving cultivated mushrooms such as champignon, shiitake, oyster mushrooms, etc. You will find details of methods for preserving mushrooms in oil and in brine on page 122.

*Serves 4*

| |
|---|
| 8 slices of Bresaola (air-dried beef) |
| 8 slices of good Italian salami (eg Felino, Milano) |
| 4 slices of Parma ham |
| 8 small artichoke hearts in oil |
| 16 small gherkins |
| a small quantity of each kind of preserved mushroom you have |

Either arrange the antipasto decoratively on each plate, or present it well displayed on serving dishes. Serve with grissini sticks.

*OVERLEAF* ANTIPASTO WITH PRESERVED MUSHROOMS

## MUSHROOM CROSTINI

### Crostini con funghi

For this recipe you will need some good wholemeal bread and some wild mushrooms, possibly a mixture. As an alternative you can use some bought champignons together with some reconstituted dried ceps and morels. If using the dried mushroom version you have the advantage of being able to prepare this dish whenever you wish, and it can be very economical indeed. I have tried both versions and found them to be equally interesting.

*Serves 4*

| |
|---|
| 400g/14oz mixed wild mushrooms, cleaned and roughly chopped, or 300g/10oz champignons plus 20g/¾oz dried ceps and 20g/¾oz dried morels |
| 3 tbsp olive oil |
| 1 large onion, finely chopped |
| 50g/2oz lean smoked bacon, cut into small strips |
| 1 clove garlic, finely chopped |
| salt and pepper to taste |
| 4 large slices wholemeal bread |
| 1 tbsp chopped parsley |

Put the olive oil into a frying pan and fry the onions and bacon for 5 or 6 minutes. Add the garlic and the chopped mushrooms and continue to fry for a further 10 minutes or until the mushrooms are cooked. (If you use the dried mushrooms, soak them first in warm water for about 20 minutes, pat dry with a paper kitchen towel, roughly chop, and add to the other mushrooms. Should the mixture become a little dry add some of the water from soaking the mushrooms.) Cook until all the liquid is absorbed. Add salt and pepper, allow to cool slightly, and spread evenly on the toasted slices of bread. Sprinkle with parsley and serve hot.

## OYSTER MUSHROOM SOUFFLÉ

### Soufflé di pleurotus

Priscilla, my wife, is a very good cook. Unfortunately (or, as many friends say, fortunately), she is married to a man who cooks all the time at home, creating new recipes and improving old ones.

'After I married Antonio I relinquished my culinary duties – but not the washing up!' she says. 'I used to love cooking. However, my husband is far more adept and knowledgeable than I and I have quite rightly become the envy of my friends. "Do you have a microwave?" they ask. "No," I say with a smirk, "I have a husband!" Sometimes, though, I long for a traditional English Sunday lunch and then I set to and cook that; Christmas supper too, though to satisfy international family tastes there will be goose and a turkey.'

As Priscilla can cook perfect soufflés, I asked her to create one for this book. We ate it together with a grilled steak, but it could be eaten as an hors d'oeuvre; it is perfectly delicious.

'Having lived in France (the home of soufflés) I learned not to be afraid of experimenting with them. It is such a delicate mixture, ideal to suspend subtle tastes, and since mushrooms play a large part in our eating lives they appear frequently in autumn soufflés.

'A soufflé should be crusty on the outside and slightly runny in the centre. You can make a sauce of mushrooms or sauté some to go with it, and you can vary the mushrooms depending on what you have available. This is my basic recipe for September soufflé.'

*Serves 4*

| |
|---|
| 80g/3oz/6 tbsp butter |
| 1 onion, finely chopped |
| 1 clove garlic, finely chopped |
| 80g/3oz self-raising flour |
| 50g/2oz dried porcini, soaked in ½ cup lukewarm water and chopped finely (retain the water) |
| about 250ml/scant ½pt/1 US cup milk |
| salt and pepper to taste |
| 150g/6oz oyster mushrooms, roughly chopped |
| 3 egg yolks |
| 4 egg whites |

Preheat the oven to 180°C/350°F/Gas Mark 4. Warm a soufflé dish and butter well. Melt two-thirds of the butter in a saucepan, add the onion and garlic and sweat until soft. Add the flour and stir well, add the dried mushrooms and the water they soaked in, stir well and add the milk and salt and pepper to taste. Cook the oyster mushrooms separately in the remaining butter, sweat until soft and add to the mixture; allow to cool. Mix in the beaten egg yolks. Whisk the egg whites until stiff and fold into the mixture. Put the mixture in the well-buttered soufflé dish and cook in the preheated oven for 28 minutes. The middle should be quite soft. Most importantly, the guests must be ready and waiting!

# THE STARTERS

T he common belief that Italians eat only pasta and pizza is false. It is true that we do eat a lot of pasta, but the variety of the sauces, and of the pasta itself, is so infinite that each dish can be considered a separate speciality. Pasta is the 'carrier' par excellence for wild mushrooms, both fresh and dried: their succulent textures complement one another perfectly, and the savoury juices exuded by cooked mushrooms provide just the right lubrication. Different regions favour their own versions of home-made pasta and of gnocchi; in the north, polenta and rice make equally delicious vehicles for mushrooms. In keeping with tradition, these dishes offer a good way of 'stretching' the meagre harvest of a less-than-successful mushroom expedition or a small amount of precious dried mushrooms. At the other extreme, home-made pasta, simply served, makes the perfect foil for the luxury of a freshly grated truffle.

During the season every Italian eats dishes containing wild mushrooms or truffles at least a couple of times: it is a sort of seasonal 'must'. Although I am an ardent believer in using fresh products when they are in season, I have to admit that the sight of a steaming plate of Risotto con porcini on a cold and wet February day irresistibly recalls summer memories. Fortunately it is also traditional to preserve mushrooms by drying them, and newer freezing techniques have improved the situation immeasurably. In my restaurant I can offer dishes incorporating preserved mushrooms which to all intents and purposes are indistinguishable from fresh ones.

'I primi' are conventionally the first-course 'filler' dishes that precede the main course in an Italian meal, but they often make a good light meal in themselves. The more 'solid' pasta dishes and their equivalents are excellent accompanied by a fresh salad and washed down with some wine, and the soups are substantial enough when served with good bread.

## WITCH POT

### Zuppa di funghi misti

When you come back from one of those unproductive forays with a sparse but varied harvest representing a cross-section of the mushroom world, then this is the time to cook this soup. It doesn't matter which edible species you have collected, but you should have a good assortment of cleaned fresh mushrooms. This variety – and the cooking method, perhaps more than anything – is reminiscent of one of those witches' pots steaming on the hob creating a kind of Hansel-and-Gretel atmosphere. I find it not only mysterious but delicious.

*Serves 4*

| |
| --- |
| 250g/8oz mixed wild mushrooms (cleaned weight) |
| 25g/1oz/2 tbsp butter |
| 1 small onion, finely sliced |
| 25g/1oz smoked bacon, cut into strips |
| 1 small floury potato, finely shredded |
| 750ml/1½ pt beef or chicken stock |
| 1 small carton double (heavy) cream |
| 2 egg yolks, beaten |
| small bunch of chives, finely chopped |
| salt and pepper to taste |
| 4 slices brown bread, toasted and buttered |

Cut the larger mushrooms into chunks, but leave the smaller ones as they are. Put the butter in a two-handled terracotta pot and gently fry the onion over a moderate heat. After a few minutes add the bacon and continue to fry; next add the potato, and shortly afterwards, the stock. Now add the mushrooms to the pot, and simmer until the potato is very soft and the mushrooms are cooked. Remove from the heat and just before serving stir in the cream, egg yolks and chives. Season with salt and pepper.

Place the hot buttered toast in warmed soup plates, pour on the soup and serve.

## CREAM OF CEP SOUP

### Crema di porcini

This is one of the most delicious soups that I have ever created, and extremely popular in my restaurant.

During the season I use only fresh porcini, making use of the larger specimens, with their mature flavour that is especially suitable for soups.

I also deep-freeze large numbers of these delicacies in order to guarantee a plentiful supply when out of season. They keep so well that after thawing, they can even be sautéed when required, although a short cut in soup-making is simply to add the frozen mushrooms to the boiling stock.

The economical version of this recipe for people who don't have their own ceps is made by using cultivated mushrooms as a base and for texture, adding some dried porcini to enhance the flavour.

*Serves 4*

| |
| --- |
| 500g/1 lb fresh *Boletus edulis*, or alternatively 500g/1 lb cultivated champignons plus 25g/1oz dried ceps |
| 1 medium onion, finely chopped |
| 4 tbsp olive oil |
| 1 litre/2pt beef stock |
| 4 tbsp double (heavy) cream |
| salt and freshly ground pepper |
| FOR THE CROÛTONS |
| a nut of butter |
| 2 slices white bread |

If you are using fresh ceps, clean them and cut them into pieces. Cook the onion in the oil for 3–4 minutes, then add the ceps and sauté them for 6–7 minutes. Add the stock, bring to the boil and simmer for 20 minutes. (If you are using dried ceps soak them in lukewarm water for 10 minutes. Meanwhile, fry the field mushrooms together with the onions and then add the soaked ceps with their water and the stock. Simmer for about half an hour.)

To finish either method, take the pan from the heat and blend the contents. Then return the soup to the pan, add the cream, salt and pepper and heat slowly. To make croûtons, merely cut the bread into little cubes and fry in butter so that they become crisp and golden.

## MUSHROOM BROTH

### Acqua cotta

An extremely easy Tuscan speciality, found – with slight variations – all over the region. It is essentially an autumn dish, made when the wild mushrooms needed for this recipe are plentiful. 'Acqua cotta' literally means 'cooked water' – the simplest sort of broth.

*Serves 4*

| |
|---|
| 600g/1¼ lb fresh young *Boletus edulis* (ceps), or 600g/1¼ lb flat *Agaricus arvensis* (horse mushrooms) plus 10g/½oz dried ceps |
| 3 tbsp olive oil |
| 2 cloves garlic, chopped |
| 1 × 397g/14oz can peeled plum tomatoes |
| 600ml/1pt/2 US cups stock |
| 5 fresh basil leaves |
| salt and freshly ground black pepper |
| 4 slices toast |
| 60g/2oz/¼ US cup freshly grated Parmesan cheese |

If you are using horse mushrooms, soak the dried ceps in warm water for 15 minutes. Wipe the fresh mushrooms clean and slice them. In a large pan fry the garlic in the oil very briefly, then add the sliced mushrooms and sauté for 10 minutes or so. Add the soaked ceps and their liquid at this point. Sieve the tomatoes and add them and their juice to the mushrooms. Stir over a medium flame for 10 minutes. Heat the stock in a separate pan and when hot add to the mushroom and tomato mixture. Season with salt, pepper and lastly basil. Pour the soup over one piece of toast in each bowl and sprinkle with Parmesan.

## CEP AND BEAN SOUP

### Zuppa di fagioli e porcini

For this soup I use *Boletus edulis* (ceps) because their strong flavour improves the relatively bland taste of the borlotti beans. Ideally, fresh borlotti beans and fresh mushrooms, which both appear in the early autumn, should be used for this delicious soup, but I discovered that the soup is still very tasty using dried borlotti (which before use need soaking in water for 12 hours and then cooking for 2 hours) and dried porcini. I serve this version as a vegetable in my restaurant, reducing the amount of liquor to almost nil.

*Serves 4*

| |
|---|
| 700g/1 lb 6oz fresh borlotti beans in the pod, or 250g/8oz dried beans |
| 150g/6oz fresh *Boletus edulis* (ceps) or 25g/1oz dried porcini |
| 3 tbsp olive oil |
| 1 large onion, finely sliced |
| 1 litre/2pt beef stock |
| salt and pepper |

Shell the fresh beans and clean and slice the fresh mushrooms. Put the olive oil in a large saucepan and fry the onion over a moderate heat for 4–5 minutes. Add the mushrooms and the beans and fry for a minute or two, add the stock and boil until the beans are cooked (taste one to see). If using dried ingredients, soak the beans overnight and cook for 2 hours; drain and discard the cooking water. Soak the porcini for 30 minutes and add to the rest with their soaking water as usual. Salt and pepper to taste. Accompany the soup with toasted slices of wholemeal bread.

HORSE MUSHROOMS, *AGARICUS ARVENSIS*

## BASIC PASTA DOUGH

### Pasta all'uovo

This is the basic recipe for the pasta dough used in making tagliolini, tagliatelle, pappardelle, cappellacci and lasagne – it all depends on the way the pasta is cut once it has been rolled out.

For simple noodles to be eaten with just a little butter and some grated Parmesan cheese, a delicious variation on ordinary pasta is to incorporate about 30g/1oz dried porcini powder in with the flour so that the pasta itself is impregnated with the taste of mushrooms.

*Makes 450g/1 lb pasta dough*

| |
|---|
| 300g/10oz/2½ US cups plain (all-purpose) flour |
| 3 large fresh eggs |
| generous pinch of salt |

Put all the ingredients in a large bowl and mix thoroughly with a wooden spoon as far as you can go. Now use your hands to knead the dough on a floured work surface, adding a little more flour and working the mixture until the dough is smooth and elastic – it should take about 10 minutes. (Yes! making pasta is this simple!) Cover and leave to rest for 15 minutes.

Now with a rolling pin roll out the dough on a work surface, sprinkling flour to prevent sticking. Aim for a thickness of about 2mm/⅛ in. If you are making stuffed pasta such as cappellacci, don't allow the sheet of dough to dry, but go straight ahead with incorporating the filling. For lasagne or noodles, however, leave the pasta to dry for about half an hour.

For noodles, fold the dough into a loose roll and cut into ribbons of the desired width. Open the folds of noodles out gently and dry for another 10 minutes or so before cooking.

Allow about 1 litre/2pt water and 1 tsp salt to every 100g/4oz pasta. Put the pasta into the boiling water and stir briefly to prevent it from sticking together. Home-made noodles should take 3–5 minutes: test when you think the pasta is almost done. Just as it reaches the al dente stage, remove the pan from the heat, add a glass of cold water to stop the cooking process, leave for a second or two and then drain.

Toss in butter (or stir in a little sauce) and serve immediately with freshly grated Parmesan cheese.

## TAGLIOLINI FOR PAOLA AND INGE

### Tagliolini per Paola e Inge

One year, at the beginning of April, my two good friends Paola Navone from Milan and Inge Zerunian from Vienna, both paid me a visit at the same time. A visit from either of them is always wonderful, but that they should both arrive together is nothing short of amazing.

Furthermore, as if to add to my pleasure, they both brought presents for me, from Inge some of my beloved smoked 'Speck' from Vienna, and from Paola some wonderful fresh porcini from Milan, which at that time of the year was something totally unexpected. Paola told me that when passing a greengrocers in Milan she noticed that they were selling fresh porcini and couldn't resist the temptation to buy some for me, and as the season for porcini in Italy doesn't start until June or July I suspect that they must have come from either Morocco or Tunisia.

I dedicate this recipe with great pleasure to my dear friends Paola and Inge.

*Serves 4*

| |
|---|
| 45g/1½oz/3 tbsp butter |
| 4 tbsp olive oil |
| 50g/2oz smoked Tyrolean 'Speck' (or substitute smoked bacon), cut into strips |
| 1 clove garlic, finely chopped |
| 300g/10oz small, firm, fresh *Boletus edulis* (cleaned weight), thinly sliced |
| 1 can peeled and chopped tomatoes (Cirio brand are quite good) |
| salt and pepper |
| 600g/1¼ lb fresh tagliolini, or 400g/14oz dried pasta (eg linguine) |
| milk as required |
| 50g/2oz/¼ US cup freshly grated Parmesan cheese |

First prepare the sauce in a large casserole where later it will be mixed with the noodles. Put the butter and the olive oil into a casserole, heat until the butter has melted, and then add the 'Speck' or bacon. After 2 minutes of gentle frying, add the garlic, fry for another minute and then add the mushrooms. Stir gently and cook for a further 5 minutes on a low heat, stirring from time to time. Now add the tomatoes, salt and pepper, mix well, cook for another 7–8 minutes and set aside.

Meanwhile, fill a large saucepan with 5 litres/9pt salted water and bring to the boil. When boiling, add the pasta and stir to avoid sticking. If the pasta is fresh, cook for 3 minutes; if dried pasta such as linguine is used, then cook for 7–8 minutes. When cooked, drain, and add to the casserole with the sauce and place over the heat again, mixing the pasta, the sauce and the Parmesan cheese well to amalgamate. If the pasta is too dry, then add a little milk: the consistency of the dish should be neither too wet nor too dry.

## MUSHROOM LASAGNE

### Lasagne con funghi

This is a rather rich and relatively complicated dish to prepare. I suggest that you either make it as the pasta course of a substantial Sunday lunch, or serve it with a salad for a more casual meal.

The mushrooms I recommend for this lasagne are all boletes – *Boletus edulis* and *B. badius* are predictably my first choice, but *Leccinum versipelle*, though less tasty, is also good.

*Serves 4–6*

| FOR THE PASTA |
| --- |
| 450g/1 lb basic pasta dough (see page 36), or 300g/10oz bought lasagne |
| plenty of salted water |
| a little oil |
| FOR THE SAUCE |
| 5 tbsp olive oil |
| 1 carrot, finely chopped |
| 2 celery sticks, finely chopped |
| 2 shallots, finely chopped |
| 250g/8oz minced (ground) veal |
| 500g/1 lb very fresh *Boletus* mushrooms, cleaned and sliced |
| 1 × 397g/14oz can San Marzano peeled tomatoes |
| 100g/4oz thickly sliced Parma ham, cut into thin strips |
| salt and pepper |
| YOU WILL ALSO NEED |
| 200g/7oz Fontina cheese, thinly sliced |
| 100g/4oz/1 US cup freshly grated Parmesan cheese |

If using home-made pasta dough, roll it out to a thickness of about 1-2mm/less than 1/12 in and cut into 20 × 10cm/8 × 4in rectangles.

Bring plenty of lightly salted water to the boil, add a little oil to prevent the pasta from sticking together, put in the pieces of lasagne one at a time and cook al dente (about 5 minutes for home-made pasta, or 10 minutes for bought). Cool by running cold water into the pan, remove the pasta and lay the pieces separately on a clean cloth.

For the sauce, put the oil into a pan and fry the chopped carrot, celery and shallot for 5–6 minutes. Add the veal and stir-fry for another 10 minutes. Add the mushrooms and the tomatoes and cook for another 20 minutes. Remove from the heat, add the Parma ham and season with salt and pepper.

Meanwhile, heat the oven to 220°C/425°F/Gas Mark 7.

To assemble, put a little sauce in the bottom of an ovenproof dish. On this lay some of the pasta rectangles, spread a little sauce on these, add some Fontina cheese and then cover with some Parmesan. Repeat the layers in this order until all the ingredients have been used up. Place in the hot oven for 20 minutes. Cut into portions with a knife and serve straight away.

## TAGLIATELLE WITH TRUFFLE

### Tagliatelle con tartufi

One of the most popular and sought-after dishes in Alba is the simple combination of freshly made tagliatelle with the sophisticated rich white truffle which is found locally between October and the end of January. I do hope you have a good friend who will give you a present of one of these truffles.

To match the high quality of the other ingredients, choose only the best Parmesan.

*Serves 4*

| |
| --- |
| 450g/1 lb fresh tagliatelle made from basic pasta dough (see page 36) |
| 100g/4oz/½ US cup unsalted butter |
| 60g/2oz/½ US cup freshly grated Parmesan cheese from a newly cut Parmigiano Reggiano |
| 1 small *Tuber magnatum* (white Alba truffle) |
| salt and freshly ground black pepper |

Cook the tagliatelle until al dente – about 3–4 minutes. Drain, toss in the butter, stir in the Parmesan cheese and season with salt and pepper. Serve the tagliatelle to your guests on individual plates, shaving the precious truffle with a 'mandolino' directly on to each serving.

## CAPPELLACCI WITH MUSHROOM SAUCE

### Cappellacci al sugo di porcini

Stuffed pastas like cappellacci are a speciality of Emilia Romagna. Making cappellacci with home-made pasta requires a little patience, but the result is certainly worth while. They can be made the day before and stored overnight in the refrigerator wrapped in a clean cloth to keep them from sticking together. Here the cappellacci are filled with a meat mixture and the mushrooms enrich the sauce, but you could adapt a mushroom duxelles to make a vegetarian stuffing and serve with a different sauce – perhaps tomato.

I prefer ceps for the mushroom sauce here, but since the filling is rich, less flavoursome mushrooms such as honey fungus, black chanterelles or the combination of cultivated champignons and a few dried ceps are good alternatives.

*Serves 6–8 (makes 30–40 cappellacci)*

| |
|---|
| 450g/1 lb basic pasta dough (see page 36) |
| 1 beaten egg for sealing the cappellacci (optional) |
| FOR THE FILLING |
| 150g/5oz fresh Italian sausage, or finely minced (ground) fresh pork |
| 50g/2oz roasted hazelnuts, finely chopped |
| 4 tbsp freshly grated Parmesan cheese |
| 2 tbsp chopped parsley |
| 2 tbsp chopped chives |
| 5 grates of nutmeg |
| 1 tbsp olive oil |
| 3–4 tbsp double (heavy) cream |
| FOR THE SAUCE |
| 250g/½ lb fresh ceps |
| 60g/2oz/4 tbsp butter |
| 1 clove garlic |
| half a glass of dry white wine |
| salt and freshly ground black pepper |
| 1 tbsp chopped parsley |
| 60g/2oz/½ US cup freshly grated Parmesan cheese |

Make the pasta according to the basic recipe, and set it aside while you make the filling. Lightly fry the sausage meat or pork for a few minutes in the olive oil, then set aside to cool. In a bowl mix together all the other ingredients for the filling and add the cooled meat.

Roll out the pasta dough as thin as possible and cut into 8–9cm/3in squares. Place a level tea-spoon of the filling in the middle of each square and fold over diagonally, pinching the edges

together with finger and thumb – or sealing the edges with a little beaten egg if the pasta is dry. Then roll the triangle of sealed pasta into a sausage and bend it round to join the ends together, pressing the seal down on the work surface with your thumb.

For the sauce, slice the mushrooms and fry in butter. After a little while, add the finely chopped garlic and continue to cook for a couple of minutes more. Add the white wine, salt and pepper and let the liquid evaporate over a high flame for a minute or two. Then add the parsley. In the meantime, cook the pasta for about 8 minutes, then drain well and mix it into the sauce. Sprinkle with the Parmesan cheese and serve immediately.

## SPAGHETTI NORCIA STYLE

### Spaghetti alla norcina

Norcia is another famous Italian town in the centre of a well-known growing area for *Tuber melanosporum* (black Norcia truffle). This superb recipe, which is simplicity itself, can also be made using the French Perigord truffle, but you will need a little more of this as it is not so highly flavoured as the Norcia kind.

*Serves 4*

| |
|---|
| 400g/14oz spaghettini (the smallest size) |
| 8 tbsp olive oil |
| 2 cloves garlic, sliced |
| 4 anchovy fillets (preferably preserved under salt) |
| salt and pepper |
| 1 × 50g/2oz *Tuber melanosporum* (black truffle), very thinly sliced |

Cook the spaghetti in plenty of salted water. Meanwhile, prepare the sauce by putting the olive oil into a pan and frying the garlic until it begins to colour; then remove from the heat, discard the garlic and let the oil cool. Now add the anchovy fillets (from which you have removed any remaining bones), heat over a low flame until the anchovies are reduced to a pulp, remove from the heat and allow to cool a little. Finally add the very thinly sliced truffle, warm up and spread the sauce equally over the portions of al dente cooked spaghetti. Add salt and pepper carefully as the anchovies may be salty enough. Irresistible!

## HONEY FUNGUS SPAGHETTI

### Spaghetti con chiodini

I discovered the 'moreishness' of this recipe just last year, when, with the help of my friend Gennaro, I had a plentiful supply of *Armillaria mellea*, the honey fungus. I've tried it in many ways since, but this seems to be the best combination, leaving a completely satisfied palate afterwards. Again, the simplicity of this recipe seems to give an even greater pleasure to this dish.

*Serves 4*

| |
|---|
| 600g/1¼ lb smallish *Armillaria mellea* (honey fungus) |
| 4 tbsp good olive oil |
| 1 clove garlic, chopped |
| 1 small chilli pepper, finely chopped |
| 1 tbsp finely chopped parsley |
| salt and pepper |
| 400g/14oz spaghetti |
| 50g/2oz/½ US cup freshly grated Parmesan cheese |

Blanch the honey fungus in boiling water for 1 minute, allow to cool (discarding the water), and then separate the caps from the stalks – use these if still tender.

Put the olive oil in a large saucepan and fry the garlic and finely chopped chilli for half a minute, add the blanched mushrooms, the chopped parsley, and salt and pepper. Meanwhile, cook the spaghetti, drain, and add to the sauce, mix well, and serve with a sprinkling of Parmesan cheese over each portion.

You could go on, and on, and on eating this.

## PAPPARDELLE WITH HARE SAUCE

### Pappardelle alla lepre

I must admit that I don't know where the name pappardelle comes from. All I know is that it is a delicious form of pasta, similar to that used to prepare lasagne – the difference being that the dough has to be rolled out thinner and then cut into irregular shapes such as triangles, rectangles, etc.

The best time to make pappardelle is when you decide to roast an entire hare. You use some of the juices to lubricate the pasta, as they do in Italy, and then eat the meat as the main course. The next best thing is to use a joint of hare to contribute its flavour to a sauce containing an assortment of wild mushrooms – *Boletus edulis*, *Cantharellus cibarius*, *Craterellus cornucopioides*, etc – as in this recipe. Pappardelle is already delicious just flavoured with roast hare; with a hare sauce to which wild mushrooms have contributed their savoury aroma, it is unimaginably good.

Preparations have to start a day in advance to allow time for the hare to marinate.

*Serves 4*

| |
| --- |
| 1 × 3–400g/about ¾ lb piece of hare, eg leg or saddle |
| 400g/14oz pappardelle, preferably freshly made (see basic pasta dough, page 36), or dried |
| freshly grated Parmesan cheese |
| FOR THE MARINADE |
| juice and peel of 1 lemon |
| 1 bay leaf |
| 1 sprig rosemary |
| 1 or 2 grates of nutmeg |
| salt and pepper |
| red wine |
| FOR THE SAUCE |
| 1 clove garlic, sliced |
| 4 tbsp olive oil |
| 300g/10oz fresh mixed wild mushrooms, cleaned and sliced |
| 1 × 397g/14oz can peeled plum tomatoes |

To marinate, place the hare and the ingredients for the marinade in a ceramic, earthenware or stainless steel pan and pour over enough red wine to cover the contents.

The next day cook the sliced garlic in olive oil until just golden, add the mushrooms and the tomatoes and stir for a minute or two, add the hare with the marinade and cook slowly for 1 hour, then strain and retain liquor. Cook the pappardelle in plenty of salted water, drain and dress with the liquor. Add some freshly grated Parmesan and serve straight away.

# RUSSIAN PIEROGI

## Pierogi Russi

The Russians are great lovers of all kinds of wild mushrooms, and particularly of *byelii greeb* or ceps. I often picture vast areas of virgin Siberian forest in autumn, covered with wild mushrooms … Perhaps one day I'll see them.

The combination of mushrooms and pasta in this original Russian recipe given me by my friend Irina Holt has an almost Italian sound – pierogi resemble large ravioli – and I decided to devise an optional Italian style of serving them. The entente is perfect.

*Serves 4*

| |
| --- |
| FOR THE DOUGH |
| 230g/8oz/2 US cups flour |
| 1 egg, beaten |
| pinch of salt |
| water to mix |
| 1 egg for sealing (optional) |
| FOR THE FILLING |
| 25g/1oz dry white bread |
| a little milk for soaking |
| 1 onion, finely chopped |
| 45g/1½oz/3 tbsp butter |
| 400g/14oz mixed wild mushrooms, cleaned and chopped |
| 1 clove garlic, finely chopped |
| 20g/scant 1oz/¼ US cup white breadcrumbs |
| small bunch of fresh dill, finely chopped |
| salt and pepper |
| FOR SERVING |
| 45g/1½oz/3 tbsp butter |
| 20g/scant 1oz/¼ US cup white breadcrumbs, *or* 10–15 fresh sage leaves plus 4 tbsp freshly grated Parmesan cheese |

To prepare the dough, mix the flour, one beaten egg and a pinch of salt in a bowl with a wooden spoon, gradually adding enough water to obtain a stiff but smooth dough that you can knead with your hands. Set aside to rest for half an hour covered with a moist cloth.

Meanwhile, make the filling. Soak the bread in the milk. Sauté the onions in the butter until golden, add the finely chopped mushrooms and stir-fry until most of the water has evaporated. Add the finely chopped garlic, cook for another minute or two and remove from heat. Now squeeze the excess milk from the bread and add it to the mixture together with the breadcrumbs, the chopped dill, and salt and pepper to taste. Mix well and chop coarsely with a large knife.

Sprinkle a little flour on to a cool work surface (marble is best) to prevent sticking. Take some of the dough and roll out with a rolling pin to a thickness of 2–3mm/about ⅒in. With a wheel-cutter, cut the dough into 8cm/3in squares or into circles of the same diameter. Put a tablespoonful of the filling mixture into the centre of the square

or circle, cover with another square or circle of dough and press together, sealing all around the edge with the tip of a fork, or brush the edges with beaten egg and press the two sides together. When all the pierogi have been made, place them on a clean cloth and cover them.

To serve pierogi in the Russian style, plunge them, one by one, into a large saucepan containing plenty of slightly salted boiling water and cook for 5–6 minutes. Meanwhile, melt the butter, and fry the breadcrumbs in it until golden. When the pierogi are cooked drain and serve them on a hot plate sprinkled with fried breadcrumbs.

The Italian way of serving them would be to add the sage leaves instead of the breadcrumbs to the melted butter, and to toss the pierogi in this; serve on a hot plate with a sprinkling of freshly grated Parmesan cheese.

## CAESAR'S TAGLIOLINI

### Tagliolini con ovoli

In this combination of 'hot and cold' all the delicacy of the raw *Amanita caesarea* (ovolo) comes out under the gentle warming influence of the pasta. I use a small mushroom called *Laccaria amethystea* to decorate this dish; its beautiful lilac colour combines exotically with the orange caps of the ovoli but unless you are a real connoisseur of fungi I would advise you to use parsley for your decoration instead.

*Serves 4*

| |
|---|
| 450g/1 lb freshly made tagliolini (see basic pasta dough on page 36), or 400g/14oz dried pasta |
| 3 large caps of *Amanita caesarea* (approx 200g/7oz), very thinly sliced |
| 80g/3oz/6 tbsp butter |
| 50g/2oz/½ US cup freshly grated Parmesan cheese |
| 2 grates of nutmeg |
| salt and pepper |
| sprig of rosemary |

Cook the pasta al dente in slightly salted water; drain, but retain some of the water. Melt the butter into the pasta and add 1 or 2 tbsp cooking water, the dash of nutmeg, the salt, the rosemary leaves and freshly ground pepper. Add the Parmesan cheese and mix well. Place equal portions on to preheated plates, sprinkle the thin slices of Caesar's mushroom on top and serve straight away.

## DUMPLINGS WITH MORELS

### Gnocchi con spugnole

Morels have only a short growing season, but since they dry particularly well, you can use them at any time of the year. I made this dish with dried ones, and the result was stunning: the combination of Italian gnocchi (the famous potato and flour dumplings) with just a hint of creamy sauce and the delicious morel makes a very succulent dish indeed.

*Serves 4*

| FOR THE GNOCCHI |
| --- |
| 900g/2 lb floury potatoes, cooked and mashed while still warm |
| 200g/7oz/2¼ US cups flour |
| pinch of salt |
| FOR THE SAUCE |
| 40g/1½oz dried morels |
| 2 shallots, chopped |
| 45g/1½oz/3 tbsp butter |
| 1 × 397g/14oz can peeled plum tomatoes, finely chopped |
| 1 small carton double (heavy) cream |
| salt and pepper |
| 50g/2oz/¼ US cup freshly grated Parmesan cheese |

Soak the morels in lukewarm water for 20 minutes, or until soft and spongy, while you make the gnocchi. Knead the mashed potatoes on a work surface, adding the flour gradually until you obtain a soft but elastic dough. With your hands roll the dough into a series of 2cm/¾in diameter cylinders (sprinkle with flour to prevent sticking). Slice the cylinders of dough into chunks 3cm/1¼in long. Hold a large (preferably wooden) fork in your left hand, prongs down, and use your thumb to squeeze the chunks of dough against the prongs, one at a time, letting the gnocchi roll off on to a clean cloth. They should curl up like ribbed shells as they roll off the fork.

For the sauce, drain the morels well. Fry the chopped shallots in the butter until golden, add the morels and the chopped tomatoes and cook for a further 5 minutes. Stir in the cream and add salt and pepper to taste.

Cook the gnocchi in plenty of salted water: they are ready when they start to float to the surface. Scoop them out, drain well and mix with the sauce. Sprinkle with Parmesan cheese and serve.

## RISOTTO WITH CEPS

### Risotto con porcini

This is the wild mushroom recipe I cook most often. It is, in my view, the most satisfying dish and I always eat it as a complete meal, because it is quite substantial – and also because I always cook a lot of it!

Usually risotto is associated with the Milan and Venice regions, but Risotto con porcini is more at home in Piedmont. There are only a few restaurants where you can eat an authentic Risotto con funghi because it always takes the best part of half an hour to cook, and if you want the real thing then it has to be prepared while you wait; you just have to be patient. Of the many versions, I prefer the simplest one, in which you can really taste the mushrooms. Since this risotto is 'con porcini', it is perhaps unnecessary for me to say that it is only possible with *Boletus edulis* (or *B. badius*) though you can resort to fresh button mushrooms plus dried ceps.

There are some super-gourmets who are not happy with mushroom risotto alone, and have to shave a few slices of white truffle on top of it. The result I leave to your imagination!

*Serves 4*

| |
| --- |
| 300–350g/about 12oz firm, small fresh ceps, or fresh button mushrooms plus 25g/1oz dried ceps |
| 1 small onion, finely chopped |
| 2 tbsp olive oil |
| 30g/1oz/2 tbsp butter |
| 350g/12oz Arborio rice |
| 1.5 litres/3pt hot chicken stock or water plus 2 bouillon cubes |
| salt and freshly ground black pepper |
| TO FINISH |
| a nut of butter |
| 60g/2oz/½ US cup freshly grated Parmesan cheese |

If you are using dried ceps, put them to soak in a small bowl of water for 15 minutes. Meanwhile, slice the fresh mushrooms. Fry the onion in the oil and butter; when it begins to colour, add the sliced mushrooms and continue to fry over a moderate flame for a couple of minutes. If using the dried ceps, chop them into small pieces and add to the fresh mushrooms, keeping the water they soaked in to add to the risotto later with the stock.

Add the rice to the pan and stir with a wooden spoon for a minute or two until it is well coated with oil and butter. Add about a ladleful of stock to the rice at a time (have the stock simmering in a pan next to the risotto), stirring continually with a wooden spoon. As the rice grains absorb the liquid, add more. Continue to stir and add the stock until the rice appears to be cooked – about 20–25 minutes.

When the rice is 'al dente', remove from the heat, season, and finish by stirring in the nut of butter and the Parmesan cheese. Serve hot and, if you like, decorate each portion with a slice of mushroom.

## POLENTA WITH MUSHROOMS

### Polenta con funghi

If Risotto con porcini is my favourite choice, then a close second for certain is Polenta con funghi. This is another classical dish from northern Italy, where polenta, especially during those shortening days of autumn, seems to give a warmth and comfort to your soul!

Although a peasant dish, Polenta con funghi can also be found on more refined tables, but somehow, always in the more mountainous regions. Indeed, I can easily imagine preparing this dish on a solid-fuel stove in a country cottage in some hilly part of Britain or Sweden, having collected the mushrooms for it just at the bottom of the garden… The 'funghi' can be the classic porcini, the useful out-of-season standby of bought mushrooms plus dried ceps, or any mixture you have to hand.

I still remember going on a mushroom hunt in the hills near Ivrea when I was about ten years old. The expert with me was my father's friend. After a long walk, around lunchtime, we reached one of those friendly cottages situated just within the tree limit (at about 1500 metres), where the polenta is constantly steaming on a wood-fired stove. We selected a few of the mushrooms we had just picked, and the Polenta con funghi was before us on the table within half an hour!

*Serves 4*

| FOR THE SAUCE |
| --- |
| 350g/12oz fresh *Boletus edulis* (cep), or cultivated champignons plus 25g/1oz dried ceps |
| 1 small onion, chopped |
| 3 tbsp olive oil |
| 30g/1oz/2 tbsp butter |
| 1 small can of peeled plum tomatoes |
| salt and freshly ground black pepper |

| FOR THE POLENTA |
| --- |
| 1.5 litres/3pt salted water |
| 300g/10oz/1¾ US cups yellow polenta flour, or 1 × 370g/13oz packet Valsugana or Star polenta |
| 30g/1oz/2 tbsp butter |
| 60g/2oz/½ US cup freshly grated Parmesan cheese |

For the sauce, clean and slice the mushrooms, and soak dried ceps for 10 minutes in lukewarm water. Prepare the sauce by frying the chopped onion in the oil and butter, followed by the sliced mushrooms. Cook these two ingredients over a high flame for 10 minutes, then add the liquidized tomatoes and continue cooking for another 20 minutes so that the water from the tomatoes evaporates. When everything is fully cooked, add the salt and pepper.

For the polenta, bring the salted water to the boil. Very carefully add the flour, stirring constantly to prevent lumps from forming. Continue to stir the polenta until you see it start to come away from the sides of the pan (30 minutes if you are using ordinary polenta flour; 5 minutes for the Valsugana sort). When this happens, stir in the butter and half of the Parmesan cheese. Serve in shallow bowls, pouring some sauce into the middle of each and sprinkling the remaining Parmesan cheese over the top.

# MUSHROOM PIZZA

## Pizza con porcini

I make this pizza in the autumn using freshly gathered porcini (my favourites, with their obviously wonderful flavour), or with a mixture of different mushrooms. Cultivated *Agaricus* species offer a good alternative and make this pizza possible all year round. Or you could use frozen porcini if you have managed to squirrel some away.

*Makes 4 pizzas*

| FOR THE BASIC PIZZA DOUGH |
| --- |
| 600g/1¼ lb/5 US cups plain (all-purpose) flour |
| 45g/1½oz compressed yeast, or the equivalent quantity of yeast powder or granules: see packet instructions |
| pinch of salt |
| 300ml/16fl oz/2 US cups warm water |
| 2 tbsp olive oil |
| FOR THE TOPPING |
| 400g/14oz mushrooms, preferably *Boletus edulis* (ceps), cleaned and sliced |
| 4 tbsp olive oil |
| 1 clove garlic, chopped |
| 8 fresh basil leaves |
| 1 tbsp fresh thyme |
| salt and pepper |
| 4 tbsp freshly grated Parmesan cheese |
| a little extra oil |

Make the dough by dissolving the yeast in the warm water to which you have added the salt and olive oil. Pour the flour in a volcano shape on a work surface and add the yeast mixture drop by drop into the centre, mixing with your hands until the liquid is absorbed and the mixture forms large lumps. Knead the dough until it has a smooth texture, then roll it into a ball. Place the dough in a bowl sprinkled with flour to prevent sticking, smooth some oil over the top to prevent a crust forming, cover the bowl with a dry cloth and leave to rise for 1 hour in a warm place – not less than 20°C/68°F. Preheat the oven to 230°C/450°F/Gas Mark 8.

Meanwhile, stir-fry the mushrooms in the oil for 2 minutes, keeping the heat up high, and adding the chopped garlic halfway through. Remove from the heat and add the torn-up basil leaves.

Divide the risen dough into four and use the ball of your hand (rather than a rolling pin) to press each piece of dough out to a 27cm/11in diameter circle. Place each circle of dough in an oiled pizza pan and on it spread a quarter of the mushrooms with their oil. Sprinkle with thyme, season with salt and pepper, sprinkle with grated Parmesan and finally dribble a little extra oil over. Bake in the very hot oven for 10 minutes and serve hot.

# IN-BETWEEN DISHES

There are times when all cooks seem to run short of ideas about what to cook. I remember many instances when my mother seemed unable to decide what to make for us. Luckily, she had such a large repertoire on which to draw for inspiration that she always managed to serve us the most wonderful meals.

I find there is nothing like a mushroom to fire the culinary imagination. When you come home from an expedition with a precious harvest or have been given some wild mushrooms as a present, your first question will be – how to cook them? Whether they are the 'aristocrats' of the mushroom world in prime condition, a respectable collection of one of the more modest edible species or simply a mixed bag, it is a challenge to find ways of cooking them that will do them justice. Very often you want to create or adapt a· dish especially for them. My response to this challenge has prompted me to invent some wonderful recipes, and even the dishes that turned out not to be exceptional have opened the door for new ideas and further development. Some of them exploit the affinity between mushrooms and eggs, or just find ways of presenting mushrooms more or less on their own. The recipes in this chapter are the results of my experimentation; often the inspiration came to me while out picking the mushrooms.

'Piatti di mezzo' are 'in-between' dishes, belonging to no specific course, and as such have a certain versatility: they make good snacks, light meals or party fare, and can even be considered for an antipasto or primo course. Very often they provide the ideal answer to that question of what to cook. With the whole range of edible wild species available (often in preserved forms, if not fresh), plus the ubiquitous cultivated mushroom, there are plenty of tasty dishes to serve all the year round, and plenty to inspire further new ideas of your own.

## FRIED PARASOL MUSHROOMS

### Mazze da tamburo fritte

The caps of some large mushrooms can be a meal in themselves, sometimes even enough for two or three people.

The parasol (*Lepiota procera*) is one such mushroom. The cap and the thick but tender gills underneath form a round, flat substantial item of food, just waiting to be dipped in beaten egg, covered in breadcrumbs, and then shallow-fried until golden. It looks like an omelette and can easily cover your plate. Good fresh bread and a succulent green salad is all you need for a delicious late-summer snack.

*Serves 4*

| |
| --- |
| 4 parasol caps – each 15cm/6in in diameter |
| 3 eggs |
| 2 tbsp very finely chopped parsley |
| salt and pepper |
| 2 tbsp Parmesan cheese, freshly grated |
| breadcrumbs for coating |
| oil for shallow frying |

Clean the parasol caps, using a damp cloth to remove any dust from the top, but without washing them. Inspect the gills and check that no 'tenants' are present. Beat the eggs and mix in the parsley, salt and pepper and the Parmesan cheese. Dip the parasol cap in this mixture first and then in the breadcrumbs, making sure the whole of the cap is covered. Heat the oil and gently immerse the mushroom. Fry each one over a moderate heat until golden on both sides.

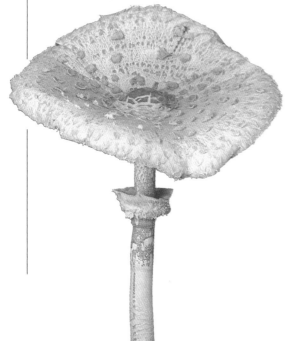

## FALSE TRIPE WITH MUSHROOMS

### Falsa trippa con funghi

This recipe is a typical result of my experiments with mushrooms. I based it on one of the dishes that my mother used to make during those lean years of the last war, when she would improvise meals using only the minimum of ingredients.

Tripe, although usually very cheap, was not available at the time, so she invented 'false tripe' made from eggs to give us an impression of the real thing. I've combined her recipe with mushrooms to make a curious but tasty dish. Any small mushrooms are suitable: I suggest *Agaricus campestris*, *Armillaria mellea*, *Cantharellus cibarius*, *Craterellus cornucopioides*, *Coprinus comatus*, *Morchella esculenta* and *M. elata*. The simple tomato and mushroom sauce makes a useful accompaniment to all sorts of food.

*Serves 4*

| |
| --- |
| FOR THE 'TRIPE' |
| 8 eggs |
| 60g/2oz freshly grated Parmesan cheese |
| salt and pepper |
| olive oil for frying |
| FOR THE SAUCE |
| 1 small onion, finely sliced |
| 60g/2oz/4 tbsp butter |
| 400g/14oz mixed wild mushrooms (cleaned weight), cut into even-sized chunks |
| 1 × 397g/14oz can peeled plum tomatoes |
| salt and pepper |
| TO SERVE |
| 1 tbsp chopped parsley |

Beat the eggs thoroughly, then mix in the Parmesan cheese and the salt and pepper. Using a small frying pan, fry as many pancake-like omelettes as you can with the mixture and cut into strips 2cm/¾in wide. Set aside while you make the sauce.

For the sauce, fry the finely sliced onion in butter. When it starts to take colour, add the mushrooms and stir-fry for 10 minutes. Add the tomatoes and salt and pepper, mix well and heat through. Arrange the false tripe on a serving dish, cover with the sauce, sprinkle with parsley and serve straight away.

## MOREL BOATS

### Barchette con spugnole

One of the advantages of this dish is that it can be prepared at any time if you use dried morels, which are available from specialized grocery shops. It is obviously better to use fresh morels, but the season for this specific mushroom is so short that most people who are lucky enough to collect any preserve some by drying them for use later on in the year. It is a lovely dish, and will be appreciated by the most critical of gourmets.

*Serves 4 (makes 8 little boats)*

| |
|---|
| 300g/10oz fresh morels, cleaned (or 40g/1½ oz dried morels) |
| 2 or 3 shallots, chopped |
| 60g/2oz/4 tbsp butter |
| 50g/2oz very thin slices of Parma ham, cut into narrow strips |
| 1 tbsp flour |
| 3–4 tbsp warm milk |
| 3 drops Tabasco |
| salt and pepper |
| 1 tbsp chopped parsley |
| 400g/14oz frozen puff pastry, thawed |

Fry the shallots in the butter until half cooked, then add the strips of Parma ham and the morels (cutting the larger ones into pieces). (If you have dried morels, soak them for 20 minutes in lukewarm water and drain, keeping the liquid, before using.) Continue cooking until the shallots are golden. Add the flour and cook for another 2 minutes. Now add enough liquid, drop by drop, while stirring continuously, to obtain a fairly stiff sauce: use milk and the morel soaking water if you have any. Add the Tabasco, salt and pepper and finally the chopped parsley. Now the filling is ready.

Meanwhile, preheat the oven to 190°C/375°F/ Gas Mark 5. Roll out the puff pastry to a thickness of 5mm/¼in and use it to line individual barquette tins. Bake blind in the moderately hot oven. Fill the boats with the prepared filling, return to the oven for 10 minutes to warm through, then serve straight away.

## FRIED MUSHROOM POCKETS

### Calzoncini fritti

The origin of the name comes from *calzone*, meaning 'trousers' in Italian. These little inside-out pizzas have their pockets full of deliciousness. They are deep-fried and fabulous for parties, hot or cold. I used cultivated mushrooms for convenience, but you could also use any wild mushrooms.

*Makes 24 calzoncini*

| |
|---|
| pizza dough made with 600g (1¼ lb) flour (see Mushroom pizza, page 48) |
| 100g/4oz smoked bacon, cut into matchsticks |
| 2 tbsp olive oil |
| 200g/7oz mushrooms, finely sliced |
| 400g/12oz/2 US cups ricotta cheese |
| 4 eggs, beaten |
| 60g/2oz/¼ US cup freshly grated Parmesan cheese |
| 4 tbsp chopped parsley |
| salt and pepper |
| 6 grates of nutmeg |
| 1 beaten egg for sealing |

Make the pizza dough as described on page 48 and leave to rise for 1 hour.

Meanwhile, fry the bacon matchsticks in 1 tbsp olive oil for a few minutes until golden and slightly crisp. Add the second tbsp olive oil and the mushrooms, and sauté for 2–3 minutes. Beat the ricotta and then mix together with the four beaten eggs; add the fried bacon, Parmesan and parsley. Stir thoroughly, season with salt, pepper and nutmeg.

Divide the dough into 24 equal pieces. Flour your work surface, roll each piece into a ball and then press out into a little circular pizza measuring 10cm/4in in diameter. Place a tablespoon of ricotta mixture on one half of the pizza and fold over to form a half-moon. Seal the join with beaten egg. When you have made all your little calzoncini, heat 1cm/½in of olive oil in a frying pan. When the oil is hot, fry the calzoncini two or three at a time, according to the size of your pan. The oil should not smoke, but be hot enough to make the calzoncini turn gently golden and crispy as they cook: they will take about 3 minutes. Drain on kitchen paper and serve straight away.

*OVERLEAF* FRIED MUSHROOM POCKETS AND FALSE TRIPE WITH MUSHROOMS

## MUSHROOMS WITH BUTTER, GARLIC AND CORIANDER

### Prataioli saltati al burro, aglio e coriandolo

The name 'prataioli' means field mushrooms, but the seasonings in this recipe complement cultivated mushrooms just as well. Try to find buttons that are still closed to make a good crunchy texture when sautéed. You can also cook other types of wild mushrooms this way – ceps, chanterelles, horn of plenty and so on. This makes the ideal vegetable accompaniment to Saltimbocca di pollo.

*Serves 4*

| |
|---|
| 350g/¾ lb mushrooms |
| 60g/2oz/4 tbsp unsalted butter |
| 1 clove garlic, chopped |
| 3 tbsp chopped coriander |
| salt and pepper |

If using button mushrooms, slice each one into three. Heat the butter until it fizzes, add the mushrooms, and fry over a fierce heat until golden at the edges and all moisture has evaporated. Now add the chopped garlic, fry for only a minute, sprinkle with coriander and season with salt and pepper. Serve immediately.

## STUFFED MUSHROOMS

### Funghi ripieni

For this recipe you can use open *Agaricus* mushrooms, wild or cultivated, or you can choose small parasol mushrooms (*Lepiota procera*) or even blewits (*Lepista nuda*). The basic stuffing I suggest here can be varied according to the ingredients you have to hand: try adding different herbs, onion, a little chopped ham, and so on.

*Serves 4*

| |
|---|
| 4 large open mushrooms |
| 1 egg |
| 1 small ripe tomato, skinned and chopped |
| 25g/1oz fresh bread |
| 4 tbsp freshly grated Parmesan cheese |
| 1 clove garlic, chopped |
| 1 tbsp finely chopped parsley |
| salt and pepper |
| 3 tbsp olive oil |
| 1 tbsp dry breadcrumbs |

Preheat the oven to 220°C/425°F/Gas Mark 7. Detach the mushroom stalks and chop them coarsely. Prepare the filling: first beat the egg and add to it the chopped mushroom stalks, the chopped tomato, the roughly broken up bread, the cheese, garlic, parsley, salt and pepper and finally 1 tbsp olive oil. Mix well together and fill the mushroom cups with the mixture. Oil a baking dish and on it place the mushrooms. Sprinkle the dry breadcrumbs over the mushrooms and trickle with the remaining olive oil. Bake in the oven for 20 minutes until golden brown on top. Serve hot or cold.

## CUTLETS OF LACTARIUS

### Cotolette di agarici

*Lactarius deliciosus* (saffron milk cap) is one of a very few mushrooms which retain some crunchiness after cooking: I use it because you can feel some resistance when you bite into it. Cutlets made with this mushroom are an alternative to the famous nut cutlets of vegetarian fare.

*Serves 4*

| |
|---|
| 500g/1 lb *Lactarius deliciosus*, cleaned |
| 60g/2oz/4 tbsp butter |
| 1 big potato, cooked |
| 1 tbsp plain (all-purpose) flour |
| 2 eggs, beaten |
| 1 tbsp finely chopped parsley |
| 60g/2oz/½ US cup freshly grated Parmesan cheese |
| salt and pepper |
| breadcrumbs for coating |
| oil for frying |

Cut the mushrooms in small strips and blanch for 1 minute. Drain well, discarding the water. Fry them in the butter until dry. Mash the cooked potato, add the flour, 1 beaten egg, parsley, cheese, salt and pepper to taste and the mushrooms. Mix well, divide into 8 portions and form into balls with your hands. Flatten into cutlets, dip into the second beaten egg and roll in the breadcrumbs. Fry till golden brown on each side and serve hot.

## CHANTERELLES IN A LITTLE SAUCE

### Cantarelli in salsina

The 'little' sauce of the title refers not to quantity, but to the simplicity with which the recipe came about.

It reminds me of an occasion at the end of June when my wife and I went out into the country with that dismal feeling of 'just another day'. All of a sudden the rain stopped, the clouds parted and the sun broke through. As luck would have it, we found ourselves very close to a place where we can usually gather a few mushrooms. The only ones my wife could find happened to be her favourites anyway – chanterelles, and she managed to collect just enough for two good portions.

On our arrival back home, we were faced with the problem of how to combine the chanterelles with the lobster that we had intended having for our meal. We decided that simplest is best, since after our country walk we were both tired and didn't wish to spend too much time preparing our meal. The chanterelles were served as first course, the lobster was boiled and eaten just with lemon and a little olive oil, and we ate some freshly boiled beans with our fingers. Wonderful! We both agreed that it was the most delicious meal that we had enjoyed for a long time.

*Serves 4*

| |
| --- |
| 400g/14oz freshly picked *Cantharellus cibarius* (chanterelles), cleaned |
| 30g/1oz/2 tbsp butter |
| 2 tbsp olive oil |
| 2 small shallots, finely chopped |
| 1 tbsp flour |
| 2 tbsp milk |
| salt and pepper to taste |
| 1 tbsp finely chopped parsley |

Put the butter and the olive oil into a pan and fry the chopped shallots. Add the chanterelles, which will almost immediately start to exude a lot of liquid. Stir and cook the chanterelles for 2–3 minutes. Add the flour, stir a little more, and add the milk, which will make a silky, delicate sauce. Add the salt and pepper and the parsley. Empty the entire contents into a serving dish and serve hot. Delicious!

## DEEP-FRIED MIXED MUSHROOMS

### Fritto misto di funghi

As the title suggests, all the edible mushrooms you can lay your hands on are good for this dish, but especially all the *Agaricus* species, all the boletes including *Leccinum versipelle*, plus *Cantharellus cibarius*, *Craterellus cornucopioides*, *Coprinus comatus*, *Lactarius deliciosus*, *Langermannia gigantea*, *Lepiota procera*, *Pleurotus cornucopiae* and *P. ostreatus* and many more. The more different species you can combine, the better. The principle is similar to the famous fritto misto of vegetables or seafood.

*Serves 6 or more*

| |
| --- |
| 900g/2 lb mixed wild mushrooms (cleaned weight) |
| 4 eggs |
| salt and pepper |
| plenty of oil for deep frying |
| breadcrumbs for coating |
| 3 lemons, quartered |

Clean thoroughly and cut the larger mushroom specimens into mouthful-sized chunks; leave the small ones whole. Beat the eggs, adding salt and pepper to taste. Pour some oil into a large frying pan to a depth of at least 2cm/¾ in and heat. Dip the mushrooms in the egg batter, allow the surplus to run off, and roll in the breadcrumbs. Place gently into the hot frying oil and fry in batches until crispy all over. Serve on a large plate, arranging them with quarters of lemon.

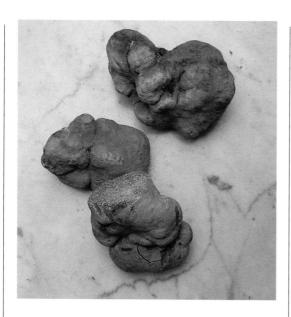

## FONDUE WITH TRUFFLE

### Fonduta con tartufi

This classic Piedmontese dish combines the excellent Fontina cheese from the Val d'Aosta with those jewels of nature – white Alba truffles. Cheese is often too strongly flavoured to be a good partner for mushrooms, but mild fontina is delicate enough to make a perfect vehicle for the fragrant truffle. If you can get hold of a fresh truffle, you are in for a very special treat indeed. If you can't, just enjoy dipping into the cheesy fondue with plenty of good bread.

*Serves 4*

| |
|---|
| 400g/14oz Fontina cheese |
| about 300ml/½pt/1¼ US cups milk |
| 4 eggs |
| 30g/1oz/2 tbsp unsalted butter |
| 1 small *Tuber magnatum* (white Alba truffle) – optional |

Cut the Fontina cheese into very small cubes and leave to soak in the milk for at least 4 hours: the milk should just cover the cheese. Thoroughly beat the eggs. In a double boiler melt the butter, add the beaten eggs, the cheese and a little of the milk that hasn't been absorbed by the cheese. Cook together over a very gentle heat, stirring all the time, until the cheese and eggs have amalgamated into a thick cream. Pour into a heated earthenware bowl and serve at once, adding the thinly sliced truffle if you have one. Provide plenty of good bread for dipping.

## MUSHROOM QUENELLES WITH TRUFFLE

### Quenelle di funghi con tartufo

I have no twinge of conscience in borrowing the idea for this recipe from the French quenelles, which are usually made with fish (as with my salmon quenelles in the next chapter). The idea is to make something heavenly-light with a divine taste. To give the quenelles a rich mushroomy taste those particularly aromatic Italian porcini would be the ideal, but in case your *Boletus edulis* are from elsewhere, I have included some dried porcini to intensify the flavour.

*Serves 4*

| |
|---|
| FOR THE QUENELLES |
| 1 small onion, finely chopped |
| 2 tbsp olive oil |
| 200g/7oz fresh *Boletus edulis* (cleaned weight), sliced |
| 25g/1oz dried porcini, soaked |
| 200g/7oz/3½ US cups breadcrumbs |
| salt and pepper |
| 4 egg whites, stiffly beaten |
| FOR THE SAUCE |
| a little water from soaking the porcini |
| 4 tbsp double (thick) cream |
| a nut of butter |
| 1 tbsp brandy |
| salt and pepper |
| TO SERVE |
| 1 × 50g/2oz *Tuber magnatum* (white Alba truffle) or black truffle if white unavailable |

Fry the onion gently in the oil for 3–4 minutes. Add the mushrooms to the pan, sweat for 5 minutes and then set aside to cool. Reduce to a smooth paste in a food processor. Add the breadcrumbs and mix well, then season to taste with salt and pepper. Very carefully fold the beaten egg whites into the breadcrumb mixture. Use two tablespoons to form the mixture into quenelles, and put them gently into a deep tray containing warm water. Put the container over a low heat and poach gently for 20 minutes.

Towards the end of the cooking time, mix the sauce ingredients in a pan and cook for a couple of minutes until slightly reduced. Drain the quenelles, coat with the sauce and serve, grating a little of the truffle over each serving.

## SANDWICH OF PARASOL MUSHROOMS

### Lepiota farcita

In Northern Europe it is not too difficult, during the season, to collect large caps of this curious mushroom which grows quite frequently in open mixed woods and in pastures. However, if you are unable to find any parasols, try the recipe using large, flat cultivated champignons, or the large horse mushrooms that you sometimes see for sale in local markets. Depending on the size of the mushroom caps, you can eat this dish either as a starter or as a main course.

*Serves 4*

| |
| --- |
| 8 large caps of parasol (*Lepiota procera*), or 8 whole large flat champignons |
| 5 tbsp olive oil |
| 2 shallots, finely chopped |
| 1 clove garlic, chopped |
| 2 eggs |
| salt and pepper |
| 100g/3½oz/1¾ US cups fresh breadcrumbs |
| 150g/6oz thinly sliced cooked ham, cut into thin strips |
| 100g/4oz coarsely grated Gruyère or Emmental cheese |
| 2 tbsp grated Parmesan cheese |
| 2 tbsp chopped parlsey |

First check the mushroom gills for 'tenants' or dirt, and clean if necessary. (Discard the stalks of parasols.) Put 3 tbsp olive oil in a pan, fry the finely chopped shallots for a couple of minutes, then add the garlic. (If you are using champignons or horse mushrooms, chop the stalks finely and cook with the shallots and garlic.) Set aside to cool. Beat the eggs in a bowl, add salt and pepper to taste, then mix in two-thirds of the breadcrumbs, the strips of ham, the fried onion and garlic with their cooking oil, and finally the cheese and parsley. Mix well, then place a quarter of the mixture in the centre of one mushroom cap, and cover with a second cap to make a closed sandwich. Prepare the remaining caps in the same way. Grease a baking tray, place the mushroom sandwiches side by side on the tray, sprinkle with the remaining breadcrumbs, and pour the remaining 2 tbsp olive oil in a little stream over the top. Bake for 30 minutes at 200°C/400°F/Gas Mark 6.

## WILD MUSHROOM BEIGNETS

### Frittelle di funghi

These beignets are wonderful for delicious little snacks. This recipe is a particularly useful way of dealing with an assortment of different wild mushrooms. You could use a mixture of chanterelles, horn of plenty, hedgehog mushrooms, boletes, parasols, and any other edible mushrooms that you can lay your hands on. It is imperative, however, that they should not exude too much moisture when cooking, so avoid using mushrooms that you have gathered during a particularly rainy spell for this recipe.

*Serves 4*

| |
| --- |
| 4 eggs |
| 200g/7oz flour |
| 100ml/¼pt/½ US cup milk |
| salt and pepper |
| 300g/¾lb mixed wild mushrooms, cleaned and cut into strips |
| 1 small onion, very finely chopped |
| plenty of oil for frying |

Beat the eggs in a bowl, stir in the flour and the milk, then add salt and pepper to taste. Now add the mushrooms and onions and mix everything together well. Pour about 1cm/½in oil into a frying pan, bring to frying temperature and carefully add the mixture, a tablespoonful at a time. Fry the beignets gently until brown and crispy on one side, turn, cook the other side, and serve hot.

## MUSHROOM DUMPLINGS

### Pilzklösschen

During the years when I lived in Austria I had plenty of time to appreciate Viennese cooking, with its dumplings such as 'Klösse' which come in many shapes and sizes up to 'Knödeln', and which accompany all sorts of dishes, savoury and sweet alike. Although this recipe is inspired by Austrian reminiscences, it perhaps has as much in common with Italian gnocchi as with Wiener Knödeln. You might like to make the light tomato sauce as an accompaniment and eat these dumplings as a first course.

*Lactarius deliciosus* (saffron milk cap) gives the dish a particular crunchiness, but other firm-textured mushrooms are also suitable. I have tried the recipe with *Laetiporus sulphureus* (chicken of the woods) and it was just as successful.

*Serves 4*

| FOR THE DUMPLINGS |
| --- |
| 150g/6oz wild mushrooms, finely chopped |
| 2 tbsp olive oil |
| 100g/4oz/½ US cup butter |
| 3 eggs |
| 25g/1oz/3½ tbsp arrowroot starch |
| 1 tbsp finely chopped parsley |
| salt and pepper |
| about 200g/7oz/3½ US cups fresh breadcrumbs |
| FOR THE TOMATO SAUCE (OPTIONAL) |
| 1 × 397g/14oz can peeled plum tomatoes |
| 60g/2oz/4 tbsp butter |
| 1 clove garlic, sliced |
| 2 fresh basil leaves |
| salt and pepper |

If you are using *Lactarius deliciosus* first blanch and drain well. Fry the mushrooms in the olive oil until cooked, then set aside to cool. Just melt the butter, then beat to a smooth foam with the eggs. Mix in the starch, parsley, mushrooms and salt and pepper to taste, then add as many breadcrumbs as you need to obtain a stiff paste that is easily shaped with your hands. Set aside to rest for 30 minutes. Then take a little at a time and, with your hands, form walnut-sized dumplings. Cook in slightly salted simmering water: they are ready when they rise to the surface – usually in 2–3 minutes. Serve as they are, or with tomato sauce.

For the tomato sauce, sieve the tomatoes to remove seeds, then purée them in a food processor. Put the butter and garlic in a small pan and cook until the garlic just begins to turn golden. Stir in the tomato purée and the basil, add salt and pepper to taste and simmer for 10–15 minutes.

## DEEP-FRIED PARASOLS AND INK CAPS

### Mazze da tamburo e coprini fritti

For this recipe you will need to collect the mushrooms while they are small and the caps are still closed around the stem – in fact, they should be cut at this point to obtain the round and oval shapes required in this recipe. As always, deep-fried food has to be served immediately after cooking to retain the full flavour, so I'm afraid you have to cook them at the last minute. Accompanied by a salad, they are a very welcome snack.

*Serves 4*

| |
| --- |
| 8 small, closed caps of *Lepiota procera* (parasol mushroom) |
| 8 small, closed caps of *Coprinus comatus* (shaggy ink cap) |
| 2 eggs, beaten |
| plenty of breadcrumbs for coating |
| salt and pepper |
| plenty of olive oil for deep-frying |

First immerse the caps in the beaten egg, and then roll them in the breadcrumbs. Heat the olive oil and deep-fry the mushrooms until golden. Serve straight away, with a salad.

## MUSHROOM PURSES

### Gruzzoletti di funghi

In this recipe I've tried to capture the distinctive flavour and aroma of wild mushrooms in a container made out of puff pastry, and because the aroma in question is particularly precious, I formed the pastry in the shape of a purse. For this recipe it is preferable to use mixed wild mushrooms. If you don't have any wild ones then you can go back to the old tried and tested method of using cultivated mushrooms with the addition of some dried ceps to improve the taste.

| *Makes 4 big purses* |
| --- |
| 1 small onion, finely chopped |
| 1 clove garlic, finely chopped |
| 50g/2oz/4 tbsp butter |
| 50g/2oz Parma ham, cut in strips |
| 500g/1 lb mixed wild mushrooms, cleaned and cut into even-sized pieces |
| 1 tbsp finely chopped parsley |
| 2 fresh sage leaves |
| a few needles of rosemary |
| salt and pepper |
| 600g/1¼ lb frozen puff pastry, thawed |
| flour for rolling pastry |
| 1 egg, beaten |

First fry the onion and garlic gently in the butter, then add the Parma ham, and then the mushrooms. Cook for about 10 minutes and set aside to cool. Add all the herbs and salt and pepper to taste. Preheat the oven to 220°C/425°F/Gas Mark 7.

Cut the (thawed) puff pastry into four and roll out each one to a 20cm/8in square with a rolling pin, sprinkling a little flour to prevent sticking. Cut from one edge of each a strip about 1cm/½ in wide and set aside. Place a quarter of the cooked filling in the centre of one pastry rectangle, fold the four corners into the centre to form the shape of a purse, and then bind the top of the purse with one of the pastry strips. Repeat this procedure for the other three purses. Set them all on a baking tray, and brush each one with beaten egg. Place in the preheated oven and bake until the pastry has a nice brown colour and you can see that the purses have increased in size – about 15 minutes.

When you open your purse, the aroma will caress your nose ... ah!!

## MUSHROOM RATATOUILLE

### Ratatouille di funghi

The ratatouille principle offers a good way of cooking a miscellaneous collection of mushrooms – cultivated ones from the supermarket, wild ones from the woods, or a mixture. As usual, I would advise adding a little dried porcini (or a teaspoon of powdered mushrooms from your store of preserves) if you are simply using bought shiitake, oyster mushrooms or champignons, which might otherwise be too bland. The result will be a succulent vegetable dish to accompany meat or fish of any kind, or to eat on its own with chunks of good bread.

| *Serves 4–6* |
| --- |
| 4 tbsp olive oil |
| 1 onion, finely chopped |
| 1 clove garlic, finely chopped |
| 2 large tomatoes, chopped |
| 2 celery sticks, finely chopped |
| 400g/14oz wild mushrooms, cleaned and sliced |
| 1 biggish aubergine (eggplant), cut into small strips |
| 6 black olives, ready pitted |
| a glass of white wine |
| 1 sprig rosemary |
| salt and pepper |

Put the olive oil into a terracotta pan, preferably with a lid. (This is also an ideal dish for a solid-fuel stove where you can use a heavy cast-iron pan.) First fry the onion over a low heat and then add the garlic. When cooked add the finely chopped tomatoes, the celery, the mushrooms, the aubergine (eggplant), the olives, and the wine, then add the rosemary and salt and pepper to taste. Put the lid on and cook slowly for 30 minutes on a gentle heat.

## RICE BALLS

### Arancini di riso

At home this dish always came the day after Risotto con porcini because my thoughtful mother always produced more than was needed in order to have some left over. Otherwise, of course, you have to go through the whole process of making risotto first. This dish is ideal to serve hot or cold at buffet parties, and the rice balls can be made in bite-sized pieces. They are good reheated in the oven next day.

*Serves 4*

| 1 quantity basic Risotto con porcini (see page 44), without the butter and cheese 'to finish' |
| --- |
| 3 eggs, beaten |
| 30g/1oz freshly grated Parmesan cheese |
| salt and pepper to taste |
| dry breadcrumbs for coating |
| olive oil for deep frying |

Make the risotto according to the method on page 44, but just when it is cooked 'al dente', spread it out on a large surface to cool and dry. When cool, place it in a mixing bowl with the eggs, cheese and salt and pepper to taste. Mix well, then form the rice mixture into balls about the size of an apricot in the palm of your hand. Roll them in breadcrumbs and deep-fry until golden.

## MIXED MUSHROOM SALAD

### Insalata di funghi misti

The ideal mushrooms for this salad appear early in the season – *Pleurotus ostreatus, Laetiporus sulphureus* and the St George's mushroom, *Calocybe gambosa, Tricholoma gambosum* or *T. georgii* (I have not included a description of this succulent spring mushroom, so check its details out in another field guide). If you want to make the dish in the autumn, I suggest you combine *Armillaria mellea* and *Lepista nuda*.

The salad is delicious warm or cold, as an antipasto or a snack. I prefer it cold, served with grissini sticks or good Italian bread.

*Serves 4–6*

| 1kg/2 lb mixed mushrooms, cleaned and sliced into even-sized pieces |
| --- |
| 8 tbsp olive oil |
| 2 cloves garlic, coarsely chopped |
| 1 red chilli pepper (not too hot), cut into strips |
| 1 bunch parsley, coarsely chopped |
| salt to taste |
| juice of 1 lemon |

Blanch the mushrooms in lightly salted water until al dente, drain and cool. Put the oil, garlic and chilli in a frying pan and fry gently over a medium heat, without browning, until the garlic and chilli have just flavoured the oil. Now add the blanched mushrooms and stir-fry for 10 minutes over a higher flame. Add the parsley, season with salt and leave to cool. Sprinkle generously with lemon juice and serve.

# MUSHROOM DISHES WITH FISH

The idea of combining mushrooms and fish is not particularly prevalent in Italian cuisine: many Mediterranean fish are better suited to other treatments. Small intensely flavoured fish such as sardines, for example, call for simple cooking and a touch of acidity as a foil for their richness rather than the additional flavour of mushrooms. So it is since I left Italy that I have been discovering how well the two partners can balance one another. This is partly because it is outside Italy that I have started to experiment with certain types of fish. For instance, I find mushrooms the perfect complement to fresh salmon. The delicate but firm white flesh of monkfish, halibut, turbot and Dover sole is ideal for cooking with fragrant wild mushrooms, since a good balance can be attained both in texture and in flavour. These dishes look appetizing, too, with the shape and colour of certain mushrooms providing an attractive or even a dramatic element of contrast. The customers in my restaurant now tuck in quite happily to fish served with horn of plenty, wood blewits, hedgehog mushrooms and other unusual wild mushrooms, as well as with the perhaps more widely known morels, ceps and shiitake. And as they begin to ask as early as January when the mushroom season is due to start, I have the satisfaction of knowing how much they will appreciate the mushroom dishes that are still waiting to be invented.

## SALMON WITH CHANTERELLES

### Salmone con gallinacci

The abundance and the fine quality of the chanterelles that I was brought from Scotland one year inspired me to invent this combination, pairing the magnificent mushrooms with another excellent product from north of the border – Scottish salmon. This recipe has no place in the Italian tradition (indeed, the eating of fresh salmon can hardly be described as widespread in Italy), but what is traditional is the principle of putting together two local specialities in season. If I was cooking in Russia, for example, I would probably be combining mushrooms with sturgeon.

*Serves 4*

| 4 × 150g/6oz supremes of salmon |
| --- |
| FOR THE COURT BOUILLON |
| 1 carrot, cut in half |
| 1 celery stalk |
| 1 bay leaf |
| 1 small onion |
| 1 tsp peppercorns |
| salt |
| water |
| FOR THE CHANTERELLE SAUCE |
| 250g/½ lb *Cantharellus cibarius* (chanterelles) |
| 115g/4oz/½ US cup butter |
| 1 small onion, finely sliced |
| 1 clove garlic, chopped |
| half a glass of dry white wine |
| 2 tbsp double (heavy) cream |
| salt and freshly ground black pepper |

Fill a casserole with water to a depth of 6cm/2in. Put in the court bouillon ingredients and bring to the boil. Meanwhile, roll up each supreme of salmon and secure with a wooden toothpick or cocktail stick. When the court bouillon is boiling, add the rolled fish, then reduce the heat to barely simmering and poach for 10 minutes. The moment the fish are cooked remove from the court bouillon and put aside and keep warm.

Clean the chanterelles with a brush, only washing them if necessary. Heat the butter in a large frying pan and fry the onion; when it begins to turn colour add garlic, and after a minute the chanterelles. Keeping the heat high, fry the chanterelles, stirring gently. Then add the wine and continue to cook until most of the liquid has evaporated. Stir in the cream and season to taste. Pour the sauce over the fish and serve.

## HALIBUT WITH LACTARIUS

### Rombo con lattario

Food, in my opinion, should look pretty (though not in a 'sissy' way), but above all, the overriding emphasis must be on the taste. This recipe combines the two qualities. Halibut, with its very white, firm flesh, goes perfectly with the orange colour and the nutty taste of *Lactarius deliciosus* (saffron milk cap). The pale green sauce is not only for aesthetic reasons; the herbs that give it its colour also contribute a special delicate taste to this distinctive dish.

*Serves 4*

| 4 cutlets of halibut weighing 150g/6oz each |
| --- |
| FOR THE COURT BOUILLON |
| 1 small onion |
| 1 small carrot, cut in half |
| a few sticks of celery, coarsely chopped |
| 1 small glass of white wine |
| salt and pepper |
| FOR THE SAUCE |
| 50g/2oz/4 tbsp butter |
| 1 small onion, finely chopped |
| 300g/10oz *Lactarius deliciosus*, preferably small ones, cleaned and blanched |
| 1 tbsp flour |
| 1 tbsp chopped dill |
| 1 tbsp chopped mint |
| 1 tbsp chopped parsley |
| salt and pepper |
| 1 small carton double (heavy) cream |

Put enough water into a casserole just to cover the fish, add the court bouillon ingredients and bring to just under boiling point. Immerse the fish and simmer for 15 minutes. Meanwhile, put the butter in a pan and fry the finely chopped onion until almost cooked. Add the sliced mushrooms and cook for 5–8 minutes or until tender; remove the mushrooms and set them aside. To the same pan, now add the flour and stir for 2 minutes, then add a few spoonfuls of the poaching water, stirring until you obtain a fairly stiff sauce. Add the herbs and salt and pepper to taste and then pass everything through a food processor. The sauce should be of a pale green colour. Add the mushrooms and the cream and reheat. Take the fish out of the poaching water, place each cutlet on a plate and pour around it the sauce with the mushrooms. Some boiled new potatoes would accompany this dish perfectly.

## SALT COD WITH CEPS AND POLENTA

### Baccalà con funghi e polenta

Baccalà is the main form in which cod is pre-served and eaten in Portugal, Spain, southern France and Italy as well as in the Caribbean. Dried and salted, it is a pungent and smelly product until it is soaked in water and turned into the most delicious dishes. You need to soak the cod in water at least overnight, with the skin side uppermost; changing the water also helps the desalination process.

| Serves 4 |
| --- |
| 700g/1½ lb good white salt cod (soaked weight 1.2kg/2½ lb) |
| 50g/2oz dried ceps, soaked in lukewarm water for 20 minutes |
| 100g/4oz/½ cup butter |
| 1 carrot, finely chopped |
| 2 leafy celery stalks, finely chopped |
| 1 glass milk |
| salt and pepper |
| 1 small onion, finely chopped |
| 2 tbsp double (heavy) cream |

Put the cleaned pieces of soaked salt cod in a saucepan, cover with cold water, bring to the boil and simmer for 50 minutes. Drain and cool. Remove all bones, skin and any tough pieces, and flake the fish.

Put half the butter in a pan and gently fry the carrot and celery for 15 minutes or until soft. Add half the drained soaked ceps, finely chopped, and 2 tbsp of their soaking liquor. Reduce in a blender to a coarse pulp, and mix well into the flaked fish. Add some milk and cook gently for about an hour, or until the cod is medium-textured, and the mixture is neither runny nor solid. Adjust flavouring with pepper, adding salt only if necessary.

While the fish is cooking, in another small pan fry the onion until soft in the remaining butter, add the rest of the ceps and some of their soaking liquor, and cook gently for 10 minutes or so, to the consistency of a sauce. Stir in the cream and serve with the fish mixture and with Crostoni di polenta (see page 100).

## OYSTER VELOUTÉ WITH TRUFFLE

### Vellutata di ostriche con tartufi

The idea for this recipe came to me in one of the most famous restaurants in the south of France. I was eating oysters in a heavenly sauce: they were just warm, and basking in a fragrant eggy coating. I tried to imagine what ingredients had been used, and the following recipe is the result. I made one important addition – some white Alba truffle. This is a very sophisticated dish for special occasions.

| Serves 4 |
| --- |
| 24 large, very fresh oysters |
| 45g/1½oz/3 tbsp butter |
| juice of ½ lemon |
| small glass of white wine |
| salt and pepper to taste |
| 6 egg yolks |
| 1 × 40g/1½oz *Tuber magnatum* (white Alba truffle) |

Carefully open the oysters over a dish to collect their liquid. Filter this liquid and put it in a pan with the butter, lemon juice, wine and seasoning. Bring to simmering point (do not allow it to boil) and immerse the oyster meat for 20 seconds only, then remove the oysters and keep warm. Now whisk the egg yolks into the liquid as if you were making zabaglione: I do this over a low gas flame, but you could use a bain marie – the main thing is to work fairly fast over gentle heat, beating until you obtain a firm foamy consistency. Taste for seasoning. Place the oysters in their pre-warmed shells and serve on a plate. Cover them with the sauce and just before serving slice white truffle over the top using a 'mandolino'.

*OVERLEAF* OYSTER VELOUTÉ WITH TRUFFLE

## DOVER SOLE WITH HORN OF PLENTY

### Sogliola con trombette

In Italy, soles are small fish, best suited to frying whole. Elsewhere, however, sole (and especially Dover sole) is available in much larger sizes, giving wonderful fillets that are ideal for this recipe. Horn of plenty, which contrasts with the fish in a spectacular combination of black and white, is not a particularly common mushroom and is rarely seen for sale. If you do manage to find some, then you are in for a real treat. Since I introduced the dish to my customers, its popularity has increased more and more.

*Serves 4*

| 8 fillets from 2 × 450g/2 lb Dover soles, or 12 fillets from smaller fish (ask your fishmonger to fillet them for you) |
|---|
| 1 onion, sliced |
| a few celery leaves |
| 1 carrot, chopped |
| FOR THE SAUCE |
| 80g/3oz/6 tbsp butter |
| 300g/10oz *Craterellus cornucopioides* (horn of plenty), cleaned |
| 1 clove garlic, finely chopped |
| juice of 1 lemon |
| 1 tsp rice flour |
| a little stock from poaching the fish |
| salt and pepper |

Roll each fillet and pin with a wooden cocktail stick or toothpick. Put enough water to cover the fish into a pan, add the onion, celery leaves and carrot and bring to just under boiling point. Place the sole fillets in this water and simmer for 10 minutes – do not allow to boil. Meanwhile, in another pan melt half the butter, add the mushrooms and stir-fry for 5 minutes. Add the garlic and stir-fry gently for another 2 minutes. Add the rest of the butter, the lemon juice and the rice flour, and cook for 2 minutes. Adjust the consistency of the sauce with a little poaching water if necessary: it should not be too liquid. Add salt and pepper to taste. Remove the sole fillets, place them on warmed plates and divide the sauce and mushrooms equally. A vegetable suggestion would be some freshly boiled new potatoes and mangetout.

## SALMON QUENELLES WITH HORN OF PLENTY

### Quenelle di salmone con trombette

One master in the art of quenelle-making is my chef Santiago, who with great patience prepares the lightest and most delicate quenelles, avidly eaten by my customers. I like salmon because it gives a lovely pinkish colour to the dish – as well as for its very delicate taste. The black colour and delicate shape of the horn of plenty (*Craterellus cornucopioides*) seems to make the perfect dish not only in its appearance, which complements the pink of the salmon admirably, but also for its taste and texture.

Bear in mind that the paste for the quenelles should be prepared a day before use.

*Serves 6*

| FOR THE QUENELLES |
| --- |
| 500g/1 lb raw salmon, cleaned of all skin, bones, etc |
| 3 egg whites, stiffly beaten |
| salt and white pepper |
| 300ml/good ½ pt double (heavy) cream |
| FOR THE SAUCE |
| 1 small shallot, finely chopped |
| 50g/2oz/4 tbsp butter |
| 300g/10oz horn of plenty, cleaned weight |
| 2 tbsp flour |
| hot milk as required |
| salt and pepper |

The day before you plan to cook this dish, reduce the salmon flesh in a blender for quite a long time in order to obtain the finest grade of paste possible. Add the stiffly beaten egg white, the salt and some finely ground white pepper, and refrigerate overnight.

The following day return the paste to the processor, add the cream and mix to obtain a homogeneous and extremely smooth paste.

Using two tablespoons, form oval-shaped quenelles from the paste and gently put them in a shallow pan of slightly salted cold water. Place over a moderate heat and slowly bring the water to the boil – at which point, the quenelles will be cooked: this should take about 15 minutes. Meanwhile, prepare the sauce. Fry the shallot in the butter, add the well-cleaned mushrooms and sauté for a few minutes. (The mushrooms at this stage will be completely black.) Sprinkle in the flour, add the salt and pepper, stir well, and add, a little at a time, as much hot milk as is neccessary

to obtain a smooth, but not too thick, sauce. Cook, stirring, for 2 minutes.

Drain the quenelles and serve with the sauce and some freshly boiled potatoes, preferably new ones.

## MONKFISH WITH CHANTERELLES

### Coda di rospo con gallinacci

A real pleasure for me is the combination of a very delicate and firm fish and a very delicate but crunchy mushroom. Chanterelles are also loved for their colour, which lends to this simply made dish a certain sophistication (and considering how expensive these little mushrooms are to buy, this is fully deserved). I suggest that you cook this dish when you find some chanterelles for yourselves.

*Serves 4*

| |
| --- |
| 50g/2oz/4 tbsp butter |
| 1 small onion, finely chopped |
| 300g/10oz chanterelles, cleaned weight |
| 800g/1 lb 12oz fillet of monkfish, cleaned weight |
| salt and pepper |
| the grated peel of 1 lemon |
| 2 or 3 leaves fresh sage |
| 1 small carton double (heavy) cream |
| 1 tbsp coarsely chopped parsley |

Put the butter in a casserole and gently fry the onion until golden, add the chanterelles, the fillet of monkfish, salt and pepper and cook on a low heat for 15 minutes stirring from time to time. The fish should poach just in the water exuded from the mushrooms. Add the lemon peel, the sage and the cream and cook very gently for another 5 minutes; add the parsley and serve straight away.

## POACHED SEAFOOD WITH WILD MUSHROOMS

### Delizie marine ai funghi

In the hope of creating a more summery atmosphere, I introduced this recipe to my restaurant during the winter months – using dried shiitake mushrooms, which I obtain easily (though not cheaply) from Chinese foodshops.

This is one of those recipe themes that you can vary infinitely, using any edible mushrooms that are available during the summer and autumn seasons. The same principle applies to the seafood: you just need a selection of at least three firm-textured kinds.

*Serves 4*

| |
|---|
| 300g/10oz giant prawns (shrimp) |
| 300g/10oz monkfish (cleaned weight), cut into chunks |
| 4 fillets of sole (let your fishmonger fillet a 500g/ 1 lb sole and give you the skin and bones) |
| FOR THE STOCK |
| fish scraps (see recipe) |
| 1 litre/2pt water |
| 1 carrot, sliced lengthwise |
| 1 onion, finely chopped |
| 1 bay leaf |
| a little marjoram |
| salt and pepper |
| FOR THE SAUCE |
| 16 dried shiitake mushrooms plus 20g/¾ oz dried ceps, or 300g/10oz fresh shiitake |
| 50g/2oz/4 tbsp butter |
| salt and pepper |

First make the stock, using the prawn (shrimp) shells if you have them, the skin and bones from the sole, and perhaps another fish head that you have coaxed from the fishmonger. Cover these with the water, add the other stock ingredients and boil for 1 hour, until the stock is reduced considerably. Strain and set aside.

Meanwhile soak the dried shiitake (if using) for at least 30 minutes, then simmer in the soaking water for 30–40 minutes or until soft. Discard the shiitake stems, which are usually tough and dirty. Soak dried ceps for 15 minutes.

Use a pan that is deep rather than wide so that you will not need too much liquid to cover the fish. Melt the butter in the pan and sauté the monkfish for a minute. Add the fillets of sole (rolled and pinned with a toothpick), the mushrooms, the prawns and enough stock – to which

you can add a little mushroom-soaking liquid – to cover. Poach over a gentle heat for about 10 minutes, or until the fish is cooked: you will see that the sole becomes friable. Serve with freshly boiled potatoes, perhaps – or, better still, with buttered noodles. Salt and pepper to taste.

## EEL WITH WILD MUSHROOMS

### Anguilla con funghi

The mushroom that suits this fish perfectly is the very aromatic cep (*Boletus edulis*). I have also tried this recipe using the honey fungus (*Armillaria mellea*), with the addition of two or three little slices of dried cep to give just a hint of flavour, and the result was stunning. It is also important not to use eels that are too thick: those of about 2cm/1in in diameter are the best. As eels have to be alive when you buy them, and as they are quite difficult to prepare, I suggest that you let your fishmonger carry out this part of the operation for you.

I sometimes substitute giant prawns (shrimp) for the eel in this dish, and serve it with boiled saffron rice – giving a somewhat Chinese effect.

*Serves 4*

| |
|---|
| 300g/10oz fresh ceps, or 350g/12oz honey fungus plus 2–3 pieces of dried cep |
| 3 tbsp olive oil (not virgin) |
| 1 small onion, finely chopped |
| 1 clove garlic, finely chopped |
| 1 tbsp finely chopped fresh ginger |
| 1 tsp chopped chilli |
| 5 anchovy fillets |
| 450g/1 lb fillet of eel, cut into 5cm/2in chunks |
| salt to taste |
| 1 tbsp coarsely chopped parsley |

If you are using honey fungus, blanch them and discard the water. Soak the dried ceps in lukewarm water for 15 minutes.

Meanwhile, put the oil into a pan, add the onion and fry for 5–6 minutes, add the garlic, the ginger, and the chilli and fry for a few seconds, add the anchovies and stir from time to time over a moderate heat until they just reduce to pulp. Now add the eel and stir-fry for 5–6 minutes, add the mushrooms (with the soaking liquid if you are using dried ceps) and cook for another 10 minutes. Salt to taste, and just before serving add the parsley.

*OVERLEAF* EEL WITH WILD MUSHROOMS AND POACHED SEAFOOD WITH WILD MUSHROOMS

## TURBOT WITH HONEY FUNGUS

### Rombo con chiodini

I love combining expensive and luxurious ingredients with humble and simple ones, as I've done with turbot and honey fungus in this delicate and interesting dish. Although the mushrooms represent the simple and inexpensive part of the recipe, I seldom see them for sale and so they may be harder to obtain than the turbot – unless you have your own source of supply. When you do find honey fungus it is usually growing in abundance, so to serve this dish out of season you could resort to using mushrooms you have frozen or preserved 'au naturel' by bottling.

*Serves 4*

| |
|---|
| 4 pieces of turbot weighing 150g/6oz each |
| salt |
| 500g/1 lb small *Armillaria mellea* (honey fungus), caps only |
| 50g/2oz/4 tbsp butter |
| 1 clove garlic, finely chopped |
| 1 small chilli pepper, finely chopped |
| 1 tbsp coarsely chopped parsley |

Poach the turbot in slightly salted water, allowing it to simmer slowly for 10 minutes, then drain and put on warmed plates. Meanwhile, blanch the mushrooms in slightly salted water for 5 minutes, and drain well. Put the butter in a pan and fry the garlic for a minute, add the chilli and mushrooms and stir-fry for a further minute or two. Salt to taste, add the parsley, and serve spooned over the fish.

## RAGOUT OF PRAWNS AND MORELS

### Ragú di gamberi e spugnole

You could use fresh morels for this dish, but considering that the morel season is so short – just a few weeks in spring – it is more likely that you will include some dried ones to contribute flavour to this recipe, but will use mainly cultivated oyster mushrooms or champignons for fresh texture. Saffron rice is the perfect complement to this delicious ragout.

*Serves 4*

| |
|---|
| 16 large prawns (about 600g/1¼ lb in their shells) |
| 40g/1½oz dried morels plus 400g/14oz fresh oyster mushrooms or champignons |
| 1 small shallot, finely chopped |
| 80g/3oz/6 tbsp butter |
| juice of ½ lemon |
| 1 glass dry sherry |
| salt and pepper to taste |
| 1 tsp flour |
| 1 tbsp chopped parsley |
| FOR THE SAFFRON RICE |
| 600ml/1pt beef or chicken stock (cubes will do) |
| 240g/8oz long-grain rice |
| 2 sachets saffron powder |
| 50g/2oz/4 tbsp butter |

Shell the prawns. Soak the dried morels for 20 minutes. For the saffron rice, put the stock in a pan, add the rice, saffron and butter and simmer until the stock has been fully absorbed. While the rice is cooking, fry the shallot in the butter and as soon as it starts to colour add the chopped oyster mushrooms or the sliced champignons. Stir-fry for a few minutes. Add the morels with a little of their soaking water (strained), the lemon juice, sherry, salt and pepper. Add the prawns and cook for 5 minutes. Stir the flour in to thicken the sauce slightly, and cook for a further 5 minutes. Sprinkle with parsley and serve with the saffron rice.

RAGOUT OF PRAWNS AND MORELS

## SEAFOOD AND MUSHROOM SALAD

### Piatto estivo di pesce e funghi

Imagine one of those very hot summer days, when sitting in the shade of a pergola is just perfect. Now imagine a table, a few friends, a chilled bottle of white wine with rivulets of condensation creating strange patterns down the dark green glass, and a sumptuous plateful of this special salad. However vivid your imagination may be, you will approach the real thing when you taste this dish, which, as many others, was created by pure chance. I was preserving some wonderful specimens of oyster mushrooms (*Pleurotus ostreatus*) given to me by my good friend Gennaro as a present. I just added a tablespoonful of those pickled mushrooms to a previously prepared seafood salad and there I was, transported back to a hot summer day, sitting in the shade ... pure magic!

*Serves 6*

| |
|---|
| 450g/1 lb squid, clean raw weight |
| 6 tails of giant prawns (shrimp), uncooked |
| 450g/1 lb tails of smaller prawns (shrimp), uncooked |
| 450g/1 lb fresh langoustine |
| 5 tbsp preserved oyster mushrooms if you have them, or cook 450g/1 lb of young oyster mushrooms in 1 part vinegar to 2 parts salted water, drain and dress with olive oil |
| 2 tbsp coarsely chopped parsley |
| 5 tbsp olive oil, virgin if possible |
| 2 or 3 tender sticks of celery from the centre of the bunch, chopped in small strips |
| 1 large clove garlic, cut in 2 |
| the juice of 1 lemon |
| salt and pepper to taste |

Clean the squid, retaining the head with the tentacles and the body, but discarding the transparent backbone and the eyes. Boil the giant prawns (shrimp) in salted water for 5 minutes, then add the other prawns, the langoustine and the squid, boil for another 7–8 minutes and set aside to cool. When cool, peel off all the shells, and cut the giant prawns lengthwise into two halves. Cut the body of the squid into rings. Keep a couple of langoustines with the claws on for decoration. Put all the ingredients into a large salad bowl and dress with the olive oil, the freshly squeezed lemon juice, salt and pepper. Mix well,

SUMMER DISH OF SEAFOOD AND MUSHROOM SALAD

then put the salad into the refrigerator for 1 hour before serving. Remove the garlic before serving: it should only give a recognizable taste before it is discarded. Eat together with a slice of good bread, or with a nice new potato salad (dress it with olive oil, vinegar, mustard, finely chopped spring onions and fresh mint, a little sugar and salt and pepper to taste).

## TROUT WITH WOOD BLEWITS

### Trota con agarico nudo

Field blewits (*Lepista saeva*) are also suitable for this recipe, but you can in fact use most mushrooms with this versatile fish, which has become, through new and intense breeding techniques, the 'Cinderella' of the fish world. One wonders if the wild specimens are still around – according to David Thomas, my friend and a naturalist, they are still out there waiting to be caught, and are very tasty indeed.

*Serves 4*

| |
|---|
| 4 × 200g/7oz rainbow trout, cleaned weight |
| white flour, to toss the fish in before frying |
| 80g/3oz/6 tbsp butter |
| 600g/1¼ lb young *Lepista nuda* (wood blewits), cleaned |
| 1 clove garlic, finely chopped |
| 1 tbsp fresh sage leaves |
| 1 small glass of dry white wine |
| salt and pepper |

Salt the outside of the trout, toss them in the flour, coating them all over, then fry them in the butter until brown on both sides. Set aside and keep warm. Add to the butter in the pan the mushrooms, garlic and sage, and fry for 10 minutes over a medium flame, stirring from time to time. Add the white wine and boil briskly for a minute to let the alcohol evaporate. Salt and pepper to taste. Put the trout back in the pan to absorb the flavour of the sauce, warm up together and serve.

## TUNA STEAK WITH WILD MUSHROOMS

### Tonno con funghi

I think that the fascination that the Italians have for eating big fish such as swordfish and tuna in slices like steak has a lot to do with the fact that, some time ago, meat was much more expensive and harder to come by than those fish. I suspect that the reverse is true nowadays.

The delicacy of a slice of fresh tuna fish, just grilled or fried in olive oil and accompanied by some mixed wild mushrooms, has to be tasted to be believed! This recipe is particularly delicious with *Boletus badius*, *Armillaria mellea* and blewits.

*Serves 4*

| |
|---|
| 4 slices of tuna or swordfish, boned and skinned, weighing 150g/6oz each |
| 500g/1 lb mixed wild mushrooms, literally anything you can find, or use fresh shiitake mushrooms – cleaned and cut in even-sized pieces |
| 4 tbsp olive oil |
| 50g/2oz/4 tbsp butter |
| 1 clove garlic |
| a pinch of marjoram |
| a few needles of rosemary |
| salt and pepper |

Salt and pepper the fish and fry it in the olive oil for 5 minutes on each side; take out of the pan and set aside. Add the butter, the mushrooms and the finely chopped garlic to the pan. Stir-fry for 10 minutes, add the herbs and salt and pepper to taste. Return the cooked slices of fish to the pan with the mushrooms etc. Stir in a tablespoon of water to help amalgamate the ingredients, warm up gently and serve straight away.

## SQUID WITH OYSTER MUSHROOMS

### Calamari e fungo ostrica

This is one of those delicious and versatile recipes where substituting ingredients creates four or five possible dishes of similar quality. I tried it using small fresh scallops (150g/6oz per person, cleaned weight) in place of the squid, and the result was very good. You can also vary the mushrooms: *Armillaria mellea* and *Lepista nuda* are like oyster mushrooms in texture, and work equally well.

*Serves 4*

| |
|---|
| 8 tbsp olive oil |
| 1 clove garlic, finely chopped |
| 750g/1½lb cleaned squid, preferably small (if large, cut into strips) |
| 750g/1½lb *Pleurotus ostreatus* (oyster mushrooms), cleaned and blanched |
| 2 tsp chopped parsley |
| 2 tsp chopped dill |
| 2 tsp chopped coriander |
| 1 tbsp chopped chilli pepper (not too hot) |
| 1 small glass white wine |
| salt to taste |
| 4 tbsp double (heavy) cream (optional) |

Put the oil and garlic in a shallow pan and fry gently for a minute. Add the squid and stir-fry for 8 to 10 minutes, depending on the size of the squid. Add the blanched mushrooms, herbs and chilli, and stir-fry for a further 5 minutes. Add the white wine and salt, and allow the alcohol to evaporate. Stir in the double cream (if used) and serve.

# MUSHROOM DISHES WITH MEAT AND GAME

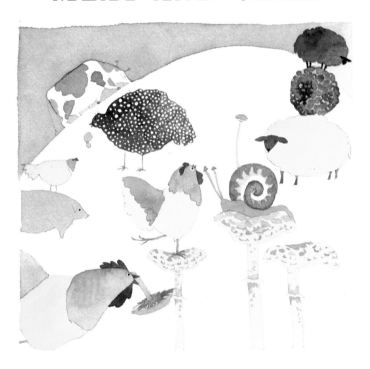

**W**ild mushrooms combine with any type of meat to produce great dishes. Mushroom sauces provide succulent accompaniments to plain grilled meat, and mushrooms are an essential ingredient of meat casseroles and stews. Whereas the more distinctive fish can clash with the flavour of mushrooms and the more delicate fish can be swamped by the pronounced-tasting ones, all kinds of red meat are substantial enough to bear up under the most pungent mushroom accompaniment. Even something as delicate as chicken can find its counterpart in subtle mushrooms like the chanterelle and parasol.

As for game, mushrooms are its natural partner. In Italy – and especially in Tuscany, where both are abundant – it is not difficult to find restaurants that offer dishes made exclusively from these two ingredients. The cuisine of most eastern and northern European countries also offers recipes based on this combination of tastes. In Britain there is no shortage of game or of hunters in pursuit of it, and this ingredient is easily available from good butchers' shops and game dealers. You have to be your own supplier of wild mushrooms, on the other hand, as well as of recipes for cooking them.

I was told a nice story by Walter Mariti, a fellow restaurateur and passionate game hunter, who attends an organized grouse-shoot in Scotland every year. One day, when they were 'walking up' birds across a stretch of moorland, they had to pass through a clump of pine trees where – much to their amazement and delight – they came across large quantities of the most glorious specimens of *Boletus edulis* or cep, which seems to be abundant in parts of the country. The grouse-shoot was rapidly transformed into a porcini-harvest, much to the consternation of their host. Local restaurateurs were then taught about the edibility of such mushrooms (which they had until that moment dismissed as toadstools) to the delight of all concerned – including, no doubt, the reprieved grouse.

## CHICKEN STUFFED WITH PARASOL MUSHROOMS

### Pollo farcito con mazze da tamburo

A nice tender chicken, boned and stuffed, is a tasty dish, but when a good wild-mushroom flavour is added to the stuffing, it becomes a culinary sensation, good to eat warm or cold. It requires some skill to bone the chicken, so perhaps you could ask your butcher to show you how it is done, or maybe to do it for you. Suitable mushrooms would include *Boletus edulis*, *Lactarius deliciosus*, chanterelles, or whatever you have available. For this recipe we use parasol caps (*Lepiota procera*).

*Serves 6 or more*

| |
|---|
| 1 good free-range boned chicken, weighing 1.5–2kg/3–4 lb |
| 4 tbsp olive oil |
| 1 onion, finely sliced |
| 300g/10oz parasol mushrooms (caps only), roughly chopped |
| 4 eggs |
| fresh breadcrumbs made from 3 rolls or 4 slices of toasted bread |
| 50g/2oz Mortadella |
| 50g/2oz/½ US cup grated Parmesan cheese |
| 3 tbsp coarsely chopped parsley |
| a few leaves of mint, chopped |
| a few grates of nutmeg |
| salt and pepper to taste |

Put the olive oil in a pan and gently fry the finely sliced onion, add the mushrooms and cook until tender, stirring from time to time; let cool. The mixture should not be too moist. Heat the oven to 200°C/400°F/Gas Mark 6.

In a bowl mix the eggs, breadcrumbs, the Mortadella cut into small cubes, the Parmesan, the parsley, mint, nutmeg and salt and pepper. Mix all together with the mushrooms; if the mixture is too liquid, add more breadcrumbs until you obtain a stiffer consistency. Stuff the chicken with the mixture and seal with wooden skewers, or by sewing up the ends with needle and thread. Grease the outside of the chicken, salt a little and put it in the oven for 1 hour. Allow to cool a little before carving, or serve cold.

## CHICKEN SUPREME WITH CHANTERELLES

### Supreme di pollo con gallinacci

For a delicate piece of chicken you need a correspondingly delicate mushroom. Chanterelles are often available in good grocery shops as well as in autumn woodland. They are ideal for this recipe, which takes little time and produces an elegant and subtle dish.

*Serves 4*

| |
|---|
| 80g/3oz/6 tbsp butter |
| 4 largish chicken breasts, skinned |
| salt and pepper |
| juice of 1 lemon |
| 1 tsp grated lemon peel |
| 2 shallots, finely chopped |
| 400g/14oz *Cantharellus cibarius* (chanterelles), cleaned |
| 2 egg yolks |
| 1 tbsp double (heavy) cream |

Melt half the butter in a frying pan, add the chicken breasts, salt and pepper and fry over a moderate heat for 10 minutes on each side. When cooked, pour the lemon juice and grated peel over the chicken and loosen any sticky bits from the pan with a wooden spoon. Set aside to keep warm.

Meanwhile, put the rest of the butter into a second pan and fry the shallots until golden, then add the chanterelles and cook for 10 minutes – they will exude a lot of liquid. Remove from the heat, stir in the egg yolks and cream, add the chicken and its juices, and mix well together. Taste for seasoning and serve warm.

## CHICKEN SALTIMBOCCA

### Saltimbocca di pollo

This is yet another extremely simple and economical dish, ideally suited to light lunches where the food is prepared immediately before eating – this should be served straight from the pan. In itself it contains no mushrooms, but it is the perfect foil for Prataioli, or *Coprinus comatus*, al burro, aglio e coriandolo (see page 54).

| Serves 4 |
| --- |
| 3 large chicken breasts |
| 100g/4oz Fontina cheese |
| 100g/4oz prosciutto crudo (Parma ham) |
| 12 sage leaves |
| 45g/1½oz/3 tbsp butter |
| salt and freshly ground black pepper |

Cut each chicken breast into four diagonal slices. Flatten the slices by lightly beating them between sheets of plastic. Slice the Fontina cheese into 12 pieces. Cut the prosciutto into pieces the same size as the flattened chicken slices. Now place on each chicken slice a piece of Fontina cheese, seasoned with salt and freshly ground pepper, and one sage leaf. Cover with the prosciutto.

In a large pan heat the butter until it fizzes, place the saltimbocca prosciutto-side-down into the hot butter and fry briefly, hardly for a minute, before turning them over. Continue to fry gently until you see the Fontina has melted and the chicken has cooked. Serve immediately, three per person, together with some mushrooms cooked in garlic and coriander.

## SUPREME OF DUCK WITH LACTARIUS

### Petto d'anitra con lattario

Duck is usually quite fatty, but if you use only the breast, it has all the flavour and no fat at all, provided you discard the skin. This dish is fit for a prince, but I think the lesser mortals among us will appreciate it in just the same way.

*Serves 4*

| |
|---|
| 4 lean duck breasts weighing 150–180g/about 6oz each |
| 3 tbsp olive oil |
| 1 small shallot, finely chopped |
| 50g/2oz Parma ham, cut in small strips |
| 200g/7oz fresh *Lactarius deliciosus* (saffron milk cap), blanched and sliced |
| 10g/½oz dried morels, soaked in warm water for 20 minutes |
| 2 cornichons, finely chopped |
| a nut of butter, rolled in flour |
| 2 tbsp dry sherry |
| salt and pepper |

Fry the breasts in the oil for 5 minutes on either side, until crispy. Remove from the pan and keep warm. Add the shallot and the ham to the pan and fry for a few minutes, then add the mushrooms, the drained morels and the cornichons and stir-fry for 5 minutes. Return the duck to the pan with any juices that have collected on the plate. Stir in the butter and flour to thicken the sauce slightly, and cook on a moderate heat for 10 minutes. Stir in the sherry and season to taste with salt and pepper. Heat to let the sherry evaporate for a minute or so, then serve warm.

## PORK FILLET WITH PLEUROTUS CORNUCOPIAE

### Filetti di maiale con pleuroto

The reason for using the best cuts of meats lies in their ease of preparation and in their tenderness. In the case of pork, in addition, the leanness of the fillet makes it easily digestible, and probably healthier as well. The fact that these cuts are more expensive than others is only to be expected; anyway, you need only buy small quantities to make a nice portion as there is little or no waste. The combination with red or yellow peppers is a very good one, and the addition of *Pleurotus cornucopiae* or, alternatively, of *Lactarius deliciosus*, makes the dish rather sophisticated.

*Serves 4*

| |
|---|
| 600g/1¼ lb pork fillet, cut into 20 slices |
| 50g/2oz pork lard |
| 100g/4oz yellow peppers, cut into small cubes |
| 100g/4oz red peppers, cut into small cubes |
| 2 cloves garlic, sliced |
| 300g/10oz small *Pleurotus cornucopiae*, or very small *Lactarius deliciosus* (blanched) |
| 1 small chilli pepper, cut into rings |
| 1 tbsp white wine |
| 1 tbsp white vinegar |
| salt and pepper to taste |

Salt the slices of meat lightly on both sides and fry them quite quickly in the lard on a lively fire for 2 minutes on each side, then put aside. Into the same pan, and over the same lively heat, first put the peppers and sauté for a few minutes, add the garlic, the mushrooms and the chilli and stir-fry for 5 minutes. Add the wine and the vinegar, mix well, reduce the heat, and continue to fry for 10 minutes. Add the meat with any juice it has exuded, taste for salt and serve straight away.

## PORK CHOPS WITH WILD MUSHROOMS

### Costolette di maiale con funghi

I only use pork in the form of chops after removing all the fat they may have. This type of cut requires more moisture and a longer cooking time to become tender. One way to achieve this is to marinate the meat in wine first. Suitable mushrooms for this dish are those that are able to be stewed and still retain their shape – morels, chanterelles, hedgehog mushrooms, small *Lactarius deliciosus*, small *Pleurotus cornucopiae*, and *Armillaria mellea*; you can also use *Laetiporus sulphureus* and *Fistulina hepatica*, cut into thin slices.

*Serves 4*

| |
|---|
| 4 × 180g/6oz lean pork chops, including the bone (the best are those with tenderloin) |
| FOR THE MARINADE |
| 500ml/18fl oz/2 US cups dry white wine |
| some bay leaves |
| 1 sprig of rosemary |
| the rind of 1 orange |
| 1 clove garlic |
| FOR THE SAUCE |
| white flour for dusting |
| 4 tbsp olive oil |
| 1 small chilli, medium-hot |
| 1 tbsp capers |
| 300g/10oz mixed wild mushrooms, made up of any of the above, cleaned and the larger ones cut into even-sized pieces |
| 6 tbsp of the marinade (including the garlic, but excluding the rest) |
| 6 tbsp stock |

Prepare the marinade by mixing the ingredients, and marinate the chops for 24 hours.

Remove the chops, pat dry, and dust with the flour. Put the oil in a pan and fry the chops over a moderate heat until they are brown on both sides. Remove from the pan and set aside. Add the garlic, the chilli, the capers and the mushrooms to the pan and sauté for a few minutes. Add the marinade and the stock, and return the meat.

Cook slowly for 40 minutes, or until the meat is tender.

## NOISETTE OF LAMB WITH PUFFBALL CUBES

### Nocciole d'agnello con vescia

It is difficult to imagine square mushrooms after all those phallic shapes. Cubing is just one way to cut up a giant puffball, which can often reach the size of a soccer ball. The cubes give a distinctive appearance to the recipe. For the combination of taste you could substitute small young *Coprinus comatus* (blanched) or *Agaricus campestris*. I have also tried this recipe with chanterelles, and it was equally delicious. To keep the puffball theme you could use about two dozen of the smaller ones, *Lycoperdon perlatum* – but make sure they are all white inside. Needless to say, when using these other mushrooms you lose the aesthetic appeal of the cubes.

*Serves 4*

| |
|---|
| 600g/1¼ lb noisette of lamb, trimmed of fat |
| 4 tbsp olive oil |
| 60g/2oz/4 tbsp butter |
| 1 onion, sliced |
| 1 × 80g/3oz slice Parma ham, cut into small cubes |
| 1 clove garlic, thinly sliced |
| 300g/10oz *Langermannia gigantea* (giant puffball), cut into 3cm/1¼in cubes, or equivalent amount of other mushrooms |
| 1 small glass of dry white wine |
| salt and pepper |

Cut the noisette into slices 3cm/1¼in thick, salt them and fry them in the olive oil for 2 minutes on each side. They should be very brown outside but underdone inside. Set aside. Put the butter in the pan and fry the sliced onion until almost brown, add the Parma ham cubes and fry for another couple of minutes. Now add the thinly sliced garlic and cook for another minute. Finally add the puffball cubes and gently stir-fry for 5 minutes. Add the wine and let the alcohol evaporate. Add the meat slices with their cooking juice, salt and pepper to taste, and serve.

## LAMB SKEWER WITH SPARASSIS

### Spiedino d'agnello con sparassis

The cauliflower mushroom (*Sparassis crispa*) is a neglected species as far as cooking is concerned. It rarely features in recipes, which is a great pity because it is a delicious and fascinating mushroom. I choose to cook it on a skewer so that the smoke produced by the charcoal grill can penetrate through the many nooks and crannies of the meandering lobes, giving a particularly good smoky, nutty flavour. For the chunks of lean lamb meat to go on the skewer I use leg of lamb cut into cubes (the butcher can do it for you) and marinated.

| *Serves 4* |
|---|
| 600g/1¼ lb lean leg of lamb, cut into 3cm/1½ in cubes |
| 4 tbsp olive oil |
| salt and pepper to taste |
| the juice of 2 lemons |
| 400g/14oz *Sparassis crispa* (cauliflower fungus) |

Marinate the meat in the oil with salt, pepper and the juice of 1 lemon for at least 4 hours.

Put some water in a pan and bring to the boil, add some salt and the juice of the other lemon.

Cut the *Sparassis* into cubes, or as near as possible, and immerse them in the boiling water for a minute just to blanch them. Drain and dry. Alternate cubes of meat with cubes of mushroom on four longish skewers and brush them with the remaining oil of the marinade. Place the skewers on a charcoal grill and turn from time to time until cooked.

## LAMB WITH HONEY FUNGUS

### Agnello con funghi

Mushrooms that go particularly well with lamb are morels, chanterelles, young *Boletus badius*, ceps, field mushrooms, *Lactarius deliciosus*, hedgehog mushrooms and, of course, the old faithful combination of cultivated mushrooms with some dried porcini. However, I think that honey fungus is one of the most successful. The meat can be an ordinary cut of lamb, provided that it is lean.

*Serves 4*

| |
|---|
| 400g/14oz *Armillaria mellea* (honey fungus) |
| 400g/14oz lean lamb, cut into small strips |
| 6 tbsp olive oil |
| 1 clove garlic, chopped |
| 1 fresh chilli pepper, chopped |
| 1 tbsp capers |
| salt and pepper to taste |

Blanch the honey fungus for 1 minute and drain well. Fry the strips of lamb in the olive oil over a high heat and as soon as the meat starts to take colour, add the mushrooms, garlic, chilli and capers. Stir-fry for a further 2 minutes, add salt and pepper to taste and serve hot.

## SPRING LAMB WITH MORELS

### Agnello e spugnole

As a tenacious supporter of cooking seasonal ingredients at the appropriate time of year, I am very fond of this recipe, which combines the tenderness of a spring lamb with the spring mushroom 'par excellence', the morel. With high-quality lamb throughout the year, you could use dried morels and cook this dish at any time, no matter what the season. I urge you to try it.

*Serves 4*

| |
|---|
| 400g/14oz noisette of lamb plus 400g/14oz fresh morels |
| *or* |
| 600g/1¼ lb lamb plus 50g/2oz dried morels |
| 4 tbsp olive oil |
| 1 small bunch of spring onions (scallions), coarsely chopped |
| 1 small sprig of rosemary |
| salt and pepper to taste |

Trim away all the fat and cut the noisette 1cm/½ in thick to obtain medallions. Salt the medallions and fry in 2 tbsp olive oil to seal them on each side (I like them when they are still pink) and set aside, keeping them warm. Add the rest of the oil and fry the spring onions for 5 minutes, add the cleaned morels and the rosemary and fry for a further 10–15 minutes, until the morels are cooked. (If you are using dried morels, soak them first until soft, and then add with some of their soaking water.) Add the meat to the morels, taste for seasoning, warm up together and serve straight away.

## MEAT LOAF IN MUSHROOM SAUCE

### Polpettone al sugo di funghi

Meat loaf does not have a high culinary reputation in some countries, but when cooked according to my mother's recipe in a delicious mushroom sauce, it becomes something special. The sauce in which it was cooked provided an excellent dressing for the pasta which was served up as a first course. Then the meat loaf, cut into slices, appeared as a tasty main course accompanied by some freshly boiled vegetables.

*Serves 8*

| |
|---|
| 1kg/2 lb minced (ground) beef |
| 150g/6oz/5 US cups breadcrumbs made from stale bread |
| 2 tbsp finely chopped parsley |
| 60g/2oz/¼ US cup freshly grated Parmesan cheese |
| salt and freshly ground black pepper |
| 4 eggs |
| oil for frying |
| FOR THE SAUCE |
| 200g/8oz thinly sliced porcini, or other wild mushrooms – substitute 20g/⅔oz dried ones only if you don't have fresh |
| 1 onion, finely chopped |
| 4 tbsp olive oil |
| 1 clove garlic |
| 2 large cans peeled plum tomatoes |
| 10 fresh basil leaves |
| salt and freshly ground black pepper |

Mix the minced meat together with the bread-crumbs, add the parsley, Parmesan cheese, salt and pepper and thoroughly mix so that the meat is well incorporated. Lightly beat the eggs and add to the meat mixture. The mixture should stick together so that you can form it into a large oval meat loaf. If you have difficulty in shaping the meat loaf and it falls apart, add a few more breadcrumbs to the mixture. (It is a good idea to fry a small meatball first to check the seasonings before you make the meat into a loaf.) In a large oval cast-iron casserole, heat the olive oil and fry the meat loaf until it is a crisp golden brown all over and retains the juices of the meat inside. Take great care not to break the loaf as you turn it in the casserole. Set the casserole aside while you make the sauce.

In a separate pan, fry the finely chopped onion in the olive oil. When the onion has become golden, add the garlic and fry only briefly before adding the mushrooms which should cook for a little while before you finally add the tomatoes, drained of some of their liquid. Cook the sauce over a medium flame for 10 minutes, stirring to break up the tomatoes. Season with salt and pepper and add the basil leaves.

Now add the sauce to the meat loaf, put the lid on the casserole and return it to the heat. Simmer gently for about 1 hour. Alternatively, you can place the casserole in a fairly hot oven (200°C/400°F/Gas Mark 6) for an hour. While it is cooking, gently turn the loaf from time to time. Remove the lid after 30 minutes to allow the sauce to thicken. When the loaf is cooked you may use the rich mushroom and tomato sauce to dress some pasta prepared in the meantime. The meat loaf should be allowed to cool for 10 minutes before it is sliced and served as a main course. You will certainly have time to allow for this while you're eating your first course of pasta.

## BRAISED BEEF WITH RED WINE AND MUSHROOMS

### Brasato al Barolo con funghi

Barolo, the king of Italian wines, is supposed to give the maximum flavour to meat and other dishes. Piedmontese beef, full of wonderful taste and tenderness, combines perfectly with the wine, producing this outstanding dish. I serve it together with some sautéed agarics or mixed wild mushrooms: see Funghi saltati in padella. However, if you want to try and improve something which is difficult to improve upon, then just add some dried porcini to the casserole with the other ingredients.

*Serves 6*

| |
|---|
| 1300g/3 lb rump steak, cut thick in one piece |
| 30g/good 1oz/2 tbsp butter |
| 3 tbsp olive oil |
| 1 bunch spring onions |
| 2 cloves garlic, roughly chopped |
| 1 carrot, split lengthwise |
| 2 celery stalks |
| small sprig of fresh rosemary |
| 2 bay leaves |
| 1 sprig of fresh thyme |
| 5 sage leaves |
| 1 cinnamon stick, 4cm/1½in long, or 1 pinch of ground cinnamon |
| the grated peel of ¼ lemon |
| 600ml/1 pt/2½ US cups Barolo wine |
| salt and freshly ground black pepper |
| 20g/⅔oz dried porcini and 10g/⅓oz dried morels |

In a heavy casserole just bigger than the piece of steak, heat the butter and oil together. When very hot add the meat and brown all over to seal in the juices – about 5 minutes on each side. Remove the meat and put to one side. Fry the onion, garlic, carrot and celery stalks for a few minutes, then add the herbs, cinnamon, lemon peel and the Barolo. Stir well, deglazing the sides and bottom of the casserole.

Now replace the steak in the sauce, season with salt and pepper, stir in the dried mushrooms and cover the casserole. Simmer very gently for 1 hour, turning the meat frequently so that it cooks evenly. Remove the lid and cook for a further 30 minutes to reduce the liquor. When the meat is cooked, remove it and set aside. Strain the sauce if you want to: you may wish to reduce it by

increasing the heat and boiling for 5 minutes or more before adding the meat.

Very gently reheat the meat in the sauce just before slicing and serving with new potatoes and, if you wish, more mushrooms – Prataioli al burro, aglio e coriandolo, or Funghi misti in umido, depending on the ingredients available.

## FILLET OF BEEF WITH OYSTER MUSHROOMS AND CHANTERELLES

### Filetto con pleurotus e gallinacci

It just happened that when I cooked this recipe for *Elle* magazine, oyster mushrooms and chanterelles were the only mushrooms I had available. The combination was an accidental one, but the result was exquisite. You could try the recipe using some other combination of mushrooms.

| Serves 4 |
| --- |
| 4 tbsp olive oil |
| 450g/1 lb fillet of beef |
| 225g/8oz mixed, cleaned chanterelles and oyster mushrooms |
| 1 clove garlic, finely chopped |
| 1 tbsp coarsely chopped parsley |
| 1 small glass of white wine |
| salt and pepper to taste |

Heat 2 tbsp olive oil in a frying pan and gently seal the beef. Add salt and pepper and cook for about 10 minutes, ensuring the beef remains pink in the middle. Remove beef from pan and set aside to keep warm. Add the remainder of the olive oil and stir-fry the chanterelles and oyster mushrooms. After about 4 minutes, when almost cooked, add the garlic and parsley. Cook for a further 2 minutes until the mushrooms are done, then add the glass of wine. When the wine has evaporated, add the salt and pepper. Combine the mushrooms and the beef and serve.

## ROAST VEAL WITH MUSHROOM SAUCE

### Arrosto di vitello con funghi

When you prepare a roast, especially one of veal with its very delicate flavour, you need a little something to go with it to create a contrast. Wild mushrooms are a good accompaniment and in this case a well-flavoured sauce is more suitable than actual pieces of mushroom – so you can use those mushrooms that you were able to dry and preserve during the summer. Bought dried porcini are also very good. In the list of ingredients I give a slightly higher quantity of meat as this dish is also very good cold.

*Serves 6 or more*

| |
|---|
| 20g/⅔oz dried mushrooms (preferably porcini) |
| salt and pepper to taste |
| 80g/3oz/6 tbsp butter |
| 1 × 1kg/2 lb piece of veal, very lean, rolled and tied |
| 2 cloves garlic, crushed |
| 1 small onion, finely chopped |
| a sprig of rosemary |
| 1 glass of dry white wine |
| a pinch of flour |

Put the dried mushrooms in water to soak for 30 minutes. Preheat the oven to 190°C/375°F/Gas Mark 5. Salt and butter the roast with about a third of the butter, place in the oven and cook at a medium heat for 50 minutes–1 hour. At this stage add the garlic, onion and rosemary and cook for another 10 minutes. Set aside and deglaze the baking pan with the wine. Drain the mushrooms and cut into small pieces. Put the remaining butter in a pan and fry the mushrooms on a medium heat for 5 minutes. Add the remaining juices from the baking dish, mix well with the flour, bring to the boil for a minute or so, and then strain. Serve the roast, cut into slices with a spoonful of the mushroom sauce.

## OSSOBUCO WITH WILD MUSHROOMS

### Ossibuchi con funghi

Ossobuco is known all over the world as that special Italian dish based on a slice of a shank of veal cut in the cross section 1½ inches thick and showing, in the middle, the round bone of the tibia with the marrow. This is exactly why it is called 'ossobuco' which means a bone with a hole. This dish is very good cooked in the traditional way but by adding some wild mushrooms to the sauce it is improved one hundred per cent.

*Serves 4*

| |
|---|
| 4 × 200g/8oz ossobuco slices of shin (cross-cut veal shanks) |
| flour for dusting |
| 4 tbsp olive oil |
| 1 small onion, finely chopped |
| 20g/⅔ oz dried porcini plus 300g/10oz fresh mushrooms |
| 10g/⅓ oz dried morels |
| 1 glass of red wine |
| 1 large can of Italian peeled tomatoes, strained of half its juice |
| salt and pepper |

Salt the marrow bones and dust with flour. Heat the olive oil in a casserole and fry the ossibuchi two at a time until brown on both sides, remove from the pan and set aside. In the same oil fry the chopped onion until slightly brown, add the presoaked mushrooms (if you use fresh ones let them fry for a little while first) then add the wine and allow it to evaporate for a minute or so. Add the tomatoes, salt and pepper to taste and cook, on a low heat, for 1½ hours.

## VEAL ROLLS WITH WILD MUSHROOMS

### Involtini con funghi

Using veal this recipe can be cooked in a very short time indeed. If you used beef instead (which would perhaps be tastier), the cooking process would be much longer. There are two tasty elements here, firstly the surprise of the filling of the meat rolls and secondly the taste of the accompanying mushrooms. It is a lovely dish to prepare and your guests will be very enthusiastic indeed. For this dish you can use chanterelles, morels, horn of plenty, hedgehog mushrooms, *Lactarius deliciosus* or any other mushroom you particularly fancy, or a mixture of the above. The only ones I wouldn't use, because they are a little tasteless by themselves, are the leccinums or the giant puffball.

*Serves 4*

| |
| --- |
| 8 thin slices of veal (weighing about 450g/1 lb), beaten flat enough to roll around the filling ingredients, plus some wooden cocktail sticks to secure them |
| FOR THE FILLING |
| 1 tbsp finely chopped parsley |
| 2 thickly cut slices Mortadella, cut into very small cubes |
| 2 cornichons, very finely chopped |
| 10 capers, very finely chopped |
| salt and pepper to taste |
| FOR THE MUSHROOMS |
| 4 tbsp olive oil |
| 1 small onion, finely chopped |
| 1 clove garlic, finely chopped |
| 1 tbsp finely chopped parsley |
| 250g/½ lb very small, cleaned, wild mushrooms |

Take care that the slices of veal to be rolled are beaten out flat between sheets of plastic on a work surface and do not show any holes. Thoroughly mix the filling ingredients and spread some evenly on each slice. Roll the veal carefully and hold firmly in place with a cocktail stick. Fry the rolls in the olive oil until brown on each side and set aside. In the same pan fry the onion first, adding the garlic when the onion is almost cooked, and then the mushrooms; stir-fry over low heat for 5–6 minutes, add the meat rolls and tablespoonful of parsley and serve hot.

## SCALOPPINE WITH MUSHROOMS

### Scaloppine con funghi

I should think that everyone knows what scaloppine are, but in case you don't I will explain. They are small flat pieces of lean veal prepared for either sautéing or frying very quickly. Owing to their size and tenderness, they can be cooked in minutes.

Scaloppine is the diminutive of 'scaloppa', which means a larger slice of the same meat. Its taste is not very intense, so one tries to compensate for this by adding other ingredients. One such flavouring is Marsala wine, creating the dish called Scaloppine al Marsala. With mushrooms, however, we do not need any other powerful ingredients. For this dish I use small specimens of *Boletus badius* (bay bolete).

*Serves 4*

| |
| --- |
| 400g/14oz veal scaloppine, beaten thin |
| flour for dusting |
| 60g/2oz/4 tbsp butter |
| 2 tbsp olive oil |
| ½ clove garlic, finely chopped |
| 2 tsp finely chopped fresh sage |
| 300g/10oz small *Boletus badius*, sliced |
| 3 tbsp dry white wine |
| 2 tbsp double (heavy) cream |
| salt and pepper |

Salt the scaloppine and dust with flour. Fry in the butter and olive oil until brown on both sides, remove from the pan and set aside. In the same pan put the garlic, the sage and the mushrooms, and stir-fry for 2 minutes over a high heat; then lower the heat, add the wine and the cream, return the meat to the pan and cook for another 5 minutes. Serve straight away. Salt and pepper to taste.

## VEAL CHOPS WITH SAUTEED MUSHROOMS
### Nodino di vitello con funghi saltati

The 'nodino', which in Italian means 'little knot', has always been, I don't know why, the name of a tenderloin veal chop which is usually cooked with sage or rosemary. If you add some sautéed cep to this already very good combination, you have a really wonderful dish.

| Serves 4 |
| --- |
| 4 tenderloin veal chops 2.5cm/1in thick |
| some flour for dusting |
| 60g/2oz/4 tbsp butter |
| 10 fresh sage leaves |
| 2 tbsp dry white wine |
| 4 tbsp olive oil |
| 300g/10oz fresh *Boletus edulis* (cep), finely sliced |
| 1 clove garlic, sliced |
| salt and pepper to taste |

Salt the veal chops and dust with flour on both sides, and fry them in butter over a gentle heat until brown. Almost at the end of the frying add the sage and wine, and set aside. In another pan sauté the mushrooms in olive oil quite quickly over a hot fire; after about 2 minutes add the garlic (almost at the end, to avoid burning it). Add salt and pepper to taste and pour the mushrooms over the veal chops, stirring well together; serve straight away.

## KIDNEYS AND MUSHROOMS
### Rognoni e funghi

I am very fond of offal and for this dish I choose calves' kidneys, which are particularly delicate in taste and very good to cook with mushrooms. Although any type of mushrooms would be good, this recipe uses horn of plenty, with its almost dry texture and intensity of colour and taste. As soon as you can collect some, you must try it!

*Serves 4*

| |
|---|
| 600g/1¼ lb calves' kidneys, cleaned of all fat and cut into thin slices |
| 3 tbsp olive oil |
| flour for dusting |
| 1 small shallot, finely sliced |
| 2 grates of nutmeg |
| salt and pepper to taste |
| 200g/8oz well-cleaned *Craterellus cornucopioides* (horn of plenty) (alternatively use 150g/6oz finely chopped champignons plus 10g/⅓oz dried morels, soaked) |
| 2 tbsp dry sherry |
| 3 tbsp double (heavy) cream |

Dust the kidneys with flour and fry them in the olive oil. When almost crispy on each side add the shallot, the nutmeg and salt and pepper to taste. Cook for 5–6 minutes, add the mushrooms and stir-fry for another 6–7 minutes. Add the sherry, let the alcohol evaporate, stir in the cream and serve straight away.

## MOREL AND SWEETBREAD PIE
### Animelle e spugnole in crosta

The inspiration for this recipe was the hors-d'oeuvre to a magnificent 'reveillon' dinner at the Imperial Hotel in Vienna, where we celebrated the arrival of 1987. I used my gastronomical x-ray eyes to identify the ingredients that left such a good impression on the palate, and created this pie based on morels and sweetbreads, both firm favourites of mine.

*Makes 4 individual pies*

| |
|---|
| 300g/10oz blanched and trimmed sweetbreads, cut into cubes |
| 50g/2oz/4 tbsp unsalted butter |
| 150g/6oz cultivated champignons plus 40g/1½ oz dried morels, soaked for 30 minutes, or 300g/10oz fresh morels |
| 2 tbsp brandy |
| 3 tbsp double (heavy) cream |
| salt and pepper to taste |
| 600g/1¼ lb puff pastry |
| beaten egg for brushing the pastry |

96

Fry the cubes of sweetbread in the butter for a few minutes until golden on all sides. Add the fresh mushrooms and then the soaked morels (if using) and cook gently for 15 minutes, stirring from time to time. Meanwhile, preheat the oven to 230°C/450°F/Gas Mark 8. Pour the brandy into the sweetbread and mushroom mixture, mix well and allow the alcohol to evaporate for a minute. Stir in the cream and add salt and pepper to taste.

Divide the mixture between four individual terracotta pie dishes. Divide the pastry into four and roll out to cover each dish, sealing the edges well. Brush the top with a little beaten egg and bake for 15 minutes or until the pastry is golden brown. Serve straight away.

KIDNEYS AND MUSHROOMS

## OFFAL WITH WILD MUSHROOMS

### Frattaglie con funghi

This dish could certainly be regarded as 'the crowning glory' for anyone who likes offal because I have brought together almost all of the possible components of this tasty subject in one recipe. As an Italian I find it difficult to understand how someone who likes liver may not like tripe, or how someone who likes kidneys may not like sweetbreads or lung. In all European cuisines, and especially that of the Italians and French, the use of offal is widespread and common. One day I would like to see many more people eating more of these tasty morsels.

*Serves 10 or more*

| |
|---|
| 200g/7oz pig's heart |
| 200g/7oz pig's kidneys |
| 200g/7oz pig's liver |
| 200g/7oz calves' sweetbreads |
| 200g/7oz pig's lung |
| 200g/7oz lard |
| 1 large glass of red wine |
| 20g/⅔oz dried porcini and 20g/⅔oz dried morels, soaked for 20 minutes and cut into small pieces (retain the soaking water) or 250g/8oz fresh mushrooms, cut into small pieces |
| 1 tube tomato purée |
| 2 whole hot chilli peppers, cut into small pieces |
| 6 fresh bay leaves |
| salt and pepper to taste |
| 4 cloves |
| FOR SERVING |
| 1½ litres/3pt stock or water |
| 8 slices of toasted wholemeal bread |

Wash all the offal under running water and remove any skin and gristle. Poach the sweetbreads in hot water for a few minutes. Cut the offal into small chunks about 1cm/½in square. Heat the lard in a heavy casserole, add the pieces of offal and fry over a strong heat, browning the pieces all over – this will take about 10 minutes. Add the glass of wine and allow it to evaporate a little before adding the mushrooms, a little of the mushroom soaking water, the tomato purée, the chillies, the bay leaves, salt and plenty of freshly ground black pepper. Reduce the heat to moderate and cook for a further 30 minutes. Leave everything to cool and set overnight.

To serve, the following day or whenever (this dish is excellent for freezing), spoon the solid mixture into a saucepan, add the stock or water and bring to the boil. The proportions are 2 heaped tablespoonsful of meat to 150ml/5fl oz/⅔ US cup of liquid. Place some toasted wholemeal bread in the bottom of a soup dish, pour the hot mixture over it and serve straight away. It is simply delicious, especially in winter; it is not really a soup, although, of course, you can serve it as such.

## HARE WITH MUSHROOMS AND POLENTA

### Lepre con funghi e polenta

Luckily, the hare, proverbially known for its astuteness, is often able to avoid being caught by swarms of covetous Italian hunters – otherwise, it would undoubtedly be extinct in Italy by now. Here in Britain, it is possible to order and buy a hare from your butcher. Hare is one item of game with an intensely 'wild' flavour, which is why a marinade is necessary – for as long as 48 hours if possible. The polenta is an irreplaceable accompaniment of game dishes in northern Italy. To justify the extensive preparations for this recipe, it may be better for you to give a small party!

*Serves 8*

| |
|---|
| 1 large hare weighing 2kg/4 lb, cut into pieces |
| flour for coating |
| 8 tbsp olive oil |
| FOR THE MARINADE |
| 500ml/18fl oz/2 US cups strong red wine, preferably Barolo |
| 50g/2oz raisins |
| 5 cloves |
| the grated peel of 1 orange |
| 10 bay leaves |
| 1 large sprig of thyme |
| 1 sprig of fresh rosemary |
| 2 cloves garlic |
| 1 tbsp honey |
| 1 bunch of celery leaves |
| 1 large carrot, finely chopped |
| 1 tsp mustard |
| salt and pepper to taste |
| FOR THE SAUCE |
| 50g/2oz dried porcini (ceps) (if you possess any fresh porcini, use 400g/14oz of them) |
| 50g/2oz/4 tbsp butter |
| 1 small onion, finely chopped |
| 50g/2oz Parma ham |

| FOR THE CROSTONI DI POLENTA |
| --- |
| 300g/10oz/1¾ US cups Star or Valsugana brand polenta |
| 1.5 litres/3 pt water |
| 30g/1oz/2 tbsp butter for frying |

Prepare the marinade ingredients, and add the hare, including any blood the hare produced when you cut it up. Marinate for at least 24 hours.

At the end of the marinating period, remove the pieces of hare from the marinade, pat dry with a cloth, salt the pieces and dust with some flour, and fry them in hot oil on all sides. Remove the pieces of hare and place them in a cast-iron pan. Pour a little of the marinade into the pan in which you have just fried the hare and deglaze with a wooden spoon. Add these to the cast-iron pan, cover the hare with more of the marinade, bring to the boil, turn down the heat and cook gently for 1 hour. Add the dried ceps and cook for a further hour, until the hare is tender.

Meanwhile prepare the polenta for making crostoni as described in the recipe for Polenta e porcini (see page 45). Pour the mixture into a tray, allow to cool and cut into slices ready to fry for serving.

After 2 hours the hare will be cooked. If you are using the fresh porcini, now is the time to add them. Fry them in the butter with the onions, add the Parma ham cut into strips, take the pieces of hare from the casserole, strain the liquid, and add to the onions and Parma ham. Stir well and simmer for a few more minutes. Season to taste, pour the sauce over the hare and serve with polenta crusts, which you make by frying the cold polenta slices in the butter until golden brown on both sides.

# FRICASSEE OF RABBIT WITH MIXED MUSHROOMS

## Fricassea di coniglio con funghi misti

This is another recipe for those times when your mushroom hunt has produced more variety and quality than quantity. The ideal would be to combine the more flavoursome mushrooms with those that offer a contrast of texture and perhaps colour. The important thing is to cook a well-balanced dish that has something for both eye and palate.

| *Serves 4* |
| --- |
| 500g/1 lb good rabbit meat, not too many bones |
| a little flour |
| 4 tbsp olive oil |
| 50g/2oz smoked bacon, finely chopped |
| 1 leek, finely chopped |
| 1 carrot, finely chopped |
| 1 glass of white wine |
| 500g/1 lb mixed mushrooms, cleaned weight, for example boletes, *Agaricus*, chanterelles, *Pleurotus*, etc |
| a little stock, if necessary |
| salt and pepper |

Turn the pieces of rabbit in flour and fry on each side in hot olive oil until cooked. Take the rabbit out of the pan and set aside. In the same oil fry the smoked bacon, the leek and the carrot for 6 minutes. Now add the wine, let it evaporate a little, and then add the mushrooms, cut into even-sized pieces. If the pan becomes too dry, add a little stock (made with a cube). Let the mushrooms cook for 10 minutes, stirring from time to time. Return the rabbit meat to the pan, heat through, add salt and pepper to taste, and serve.

## STUFFED ROAST PHEASANT

### Fagiano farcito al forno

In Italy pheasant is considered the prince of all feathered game and is consumed almost immediately it is caught, whereas in English-speaking countries it is more usual to let the bird hang and season for seven to eight days after it is killed.

This recipe calls for female pheasants, which are generally more tender and succulent than the male of the species. Accompany this dish with some beautiful yellowy-orange chanterelle mushrooms, if they are in season, or other mixed mushrooms, sautéed (see Funghi saltati in padella).

*Serves 4*

| |
|---|
| 2 female pheasants weighing about 750g/1½ lb each when cleaned |
| 2 slivers fatty bacon (if the pheasant is not sold already trussed with bacon) |
| FOR THE STUFFING |
| 1 small onion, finely chopped |
| 1 clove garlic, chopped |
| 2 tbsp olive oil |
| 250g/½ lb minced (ground) pork |
| the livers from the pheasants, chopped |
| 2 whole cloves, crushed |
| 1 tbsp chopped parsley |
| 1 sprig of rosemary, finely chopped |
| 1 tbsp dry breadcrumbs |
| ¼ nutmeg, grated |
| 10g/⅓oz dried ceps and 5g/⅙oz dried morels, both soaked for 20 minutes and then finely chopped |
| a nut of butter |
| FOR THE SAUCE |
| 45g/1½oz/3 tbsp butter |
| ½ tbsp flour |
| half a glass of white wine |
| salt and freshly ground black pepper |

Thoroughly clean the pheasants. Preheat the oven to 200°C/400°F/Gas Mark 6.

To make the stuffing, fry the chopped onion and garlic in the oil and add to it the chopped pheasant livers and the minced pork, plus the crushed cloves. Continue cooking together for 8 minutes, then remove the mixture from the flame. Let it cool down and then add the chopped parsley, rosemary, breadcrumbs, nutmeg and the mushrooms. Mix all these ingredients together thoroughly and season with salt and pepper.

Stuff the pheasants with this mixture and tie in the stuffing with the pieces of bacon. Place a knob of butter on each bird and cook in the hot oven for 1½ hours. Baste the birds every now and again with the juices in the baking pan. When cooked, remove from the pan and keep hot.

To prepare the sauce, heat up the pheasant juices in the roasting pan, skim away any excess bacon fat, then stir in the butter and the flour. After a few minutes, pour in the wine and continue to stir over the heat for a minute or two. Season with salt and pepper.

To serve, cut the pheasants into quarters, with the stuffing, and pour the sauce over.

## PARTRIDGE WITH WOOD BLEWITS

### Pernici con Lepista nuda

Wood blewits and field blewits are excellent mushrooms and are quite common during the autumn and early winter. I personally have never seen blewits for sale in markets or specialist shops, which is surprising owing to the abundance of these wonderful mushrooms when in season. Though they have a strong and perfumed taste, they do not need to be cooked in any particular way. I combine them with the partridges in a very simple way called 'trifolati' which means to sauté in butter with garlic and parsley.

*Serves 4*

| |
|---|
| 2 tbsp olive oil |
| 4 partridges |
| salt and pepper plus a little sweet paprika |
| half a glass of dry white wine |
| 60g/2oz/4 tbsp butter |
| 500g/1 lb *Lepista nuda* or *L. saeva* (wood or field blewits), cleaned |
| 1 clove garlic, finely chopped |
| 2 tbsp finely chopped parsley |

Put some olive oil into an iron ovenproof pan. Sprinkle the partridges inside and out with some salt, pepper and paprika, and fry them on each side for 5 minutes, then pour the wine over them and complete cooking in a very hot oven. Meanwhile, put the butter in a frying pan and when hot add the mushrooms (the larger ones cut into four), and stir-fry for 10 minutes. Almost at the end, add the garlic and fry for another couple of minutes. Serve the partridges surrounded by mushrooms and sprinkled with parsley.

*OVERLEAF* HUNTERS' CASSEROLE AND FRICASSEE OF RABBIT WITH MIXED MUSHROOMS

## SUPREME OF PHEASANT WITH TRUFFLE

### Supreme di fagiano al tartufo

It may appear wasteful to use only the 'supreme' of a bird such as pheasant, but this is not so, because with the rest of the bird (including the bones), it is possible to prepare the most wonderful game soup: boil the remainder of the pheasant with a finely chopped carrot, some juniper berries, some rosemary, a finely chopped leek, and add 2 or 3 slices of dried porcini. Cook for 1½ hours and enrich with a small glass of port and, if you wish, some cream.

*Serves 4*

| |
|---|
| 4 pheasant breasts, with skin |
| the livers from the two birds |
| 1 small sachet of saffron powder |
| ¼ tsp mushroom powder |
| 1 small onion, finely chopped |
| 2 tbsp olive oil |
| 1 small glass of whisky |
| 1 small sprig of rosemary |
| 2 bay leaves |
| 2 sage leaves |
| 50g/2oz/2 tbsp butter |
| salt and pepper to taste |
| 1 × 50g/2oz *Tuber magnatum* (white Alba truffle) |

Place the pheasant breasts and livers with the saffron, mushroom powder, chopped onion, olive oil, whisky, rosemary, sage and bay leaves all together in a pan to marinate for a few hours. Then remove the breasts from the marinade and pat dry, place half of the butter in a pan and fry the breasts until golden on each side, then remove from the pan. Into the same pan put the livers; remove the sage, rosemary and bay leaves from the marinade and pour this into the pan. Cook this gently for 10 minutes and then liquidize in a blender. Put the rest of the butter into the same casserole, let it liquefy, add the processed liver mixture. Add salt and pepper to taste and add the pheasant breasts to warm up. Serve on individual plates, shaving a quarter of the truffle over each of them when on the table.

## GAME AND MUSHROOM PIE

### Crostata ripiena di funghi e selvaggina

I specifically created this recipe to honour the abundance of good game and wild mushrooms that can be found in my adopted country. A pie has the property to seal, within its pastry case, the aroma of its ingredients – which is released when you cut into it. It is a must in the autumn when the game season is under way and the woods seem to catch fire just before the leaves fall.

The meat in this recipe needs to be marinated for 24 hours before being cooked. The initial cooking of the pie filling can be done ahead of time, but the meat should be reheated before it is put into the ramekin.

*Makes 6 individual pies*

| |
|---|
| 400g/14oz fillet of venison, cut into chunks |
| 500g/1 lb pheasant, boned and cut into chunks |
| FOR THE MARINADE |
| 2 carrots, chopped |
| 1 leek, chopped |
| 2 sticks of celery, chopped |
| 1 small sprig of rosemary |
| 6 sage leaves |
| a few juniper berries |
| 4 bay leaves |
| salt and pepper to taste |
| 500ml/18fl oz/2 US cups dry red wine |
| YOU WILL ALSO NEED |
| 6 tbsp olive oil |
| a little white flour |
| 1 large onion, finely chopped |
| 50g/2oz lean bacon, cut into strips |
| 450g/1 lb mixed wild mushrooms containing some ceps or dry porcini |
| 600g/1¼ lb puff pastry (frozen will do) |
| 1 beaten egg |

Prepare the marinade the day before making the pies by putting the chunks of meat and the other marinade ingredients into a stainless steel, porcelain or terracotta container. Marinate for at least 24 hours.

The following day, put the olive oil into a large casserole, remove the meat from the marinade (retain the marinade), dust the meat with flour and put it into the casserole to fry. Brown the meat slightly on each side, remove from the casserole and set aside. Now put the chopped onion in the same oil, add the bacon, and fry until the onions are golden. Add the mushrooms and cook for 20 minutes, remove from the heat and return the meat to the casserole, add the marinade and cook for at least one hour over a moderate heat.

When this cooking is completed, dish out the contents of the casserole into six nice ovenproof ramekins. Roll out the pastry 5mm/¼ in thick, cut out a piece to cover each ramekin, brush the pastry with the beaten egg and cook in a preheated oven (230°C/450°F/Gas Mark 8) for 15–20 minutes.

## HUNTERS' CASSEROLE

### Casseruola del cacciatore

This is the dish I imagine my friend Walter Mariti and his fellow hunters would have cooked after changing their grouse shoot into a mushroom hunt because the wild mushrooms they found were more tempting, and easier to 'catch'. Not being in this dilemma, I propose to cook this dish for a special occasion and prepare it for at least 10 guests, as I believe the flavour of all the ingredients would develop better using this quantity.

It shouldn't be too difficult for you to find the meats – most butchers or game dealers can provide them, but the wild mushrooms may be slightly more difficult to obtain. If you are unable to find any fresh chanterelles, ceps, hedgehog mushrooms or *Boletus badius*, then buy some cultivated oyster mushrooms, champignons and shiitake and once again use the old trick of adding a few dried ceps to improve the taste. Particularly suitable mushrooms are wood blewits, parasols,

*Sparassis crispa*, horn of plenty, chicken of the woods – in fact *any* edible wild mushrooms.

| *Serves 10* |
| --- |
| 1kg/2 lb wild mushrooms |
| 10 quails, cleaned |
| 6 woodpigeons, cleaned and halved |
| 3 wild rabbits, cleaned and quartered |
| flour for dusting |
| 8 tbsp olive oil |
| 3 carrots, finely chopped |
| 3 sticks of celery, finely chopped |
| 1 large onion, finely chopped |
| 50g/2oz lean smoked bacon, finely chopped |
| 5 bay leaves |
| 1 small sprig of rosemary |
| 5 cloves |
| 1.5 litres/3 pt good strong dry red wine |
| salt and pepper to taste |

Clean all the ingredients well. If the mushrooms are large then cut them into slices; if small, then leave them whole. Dust the meat with flour and fry in olive oil until golden on each side. Remove the meat, set aside and keep warm. To the same pan add the chopped vegetables and the bacon and stir-fry for 5–6 minutes; add the bay leaves, rosemary, cloves and the mushrooms and stir-fry for another 10 minutes. Add the wine, salt and pepper and the meat, and cook on a low heat for 1½ hours or until you see that all the meat is cooked. To accompany, Crostoni di polenta is again very good; also nice are noodles or boiled potatoes.

*OVERLEAF* GRAND CHRISTMAS GAME DISH

## GRAND CHRISTMAS GAME DISH
### Grande piatto natalizio cacciagione

The idea for this dish had been in my mind for a long time; I had always intended to cook it but it is only now, with this book, that I have had the opportunity. Since this dish is meant to be prepared for Christmas, I have complete confidence in using frozen mushrooms such as ceps, chanterelles and *Lactarius deliciosus* which I collected during the summer. Have no worries about not having fresh ingredients – I believe these are as fresh as they could be.

This is a magnificent dish, both in its presentation and in its proportions, so Christmas, when you are surrounded by relations and friends, is the perfect opportunity, and the quantities are adequate for the importance of the occasion.

Buy the birds plucked and cleaned but with the giblets separate, as they are essential for the sauce.

If you don't possess a very large serving dish, perhaps you can borrow one just for the occasion from your local restaurant. The presentation of this dish should be as majestic as possible. Happy Christmas!

### Serves 12 or more

| |
| --- |
| 1 large duck, 4 pheasants, 8 woodpigeon or grouse, 10 partridges, 12 quail (keep the livers of all the birds) |
| 5 tbsp olive oil |
| 140g/5oz/10 tbsp butter |
| 1 large onion, finely sliced |
| 4 cloves garlic, finely sliced |
| 2kg/4 lb small *Boletus edulis* (ceps) |
| 500g/1 lb *Cantharellus cibarius* (chanterelles) |
| 500g/1 lb *Lactarius deliciosus* |
| some rosemary twigs |
| 1 bunch of sage |
| salt and pepper to taste |
| some nutmeg |
| 1 bunch of chives finely chopped |

Salt and pepper the birds inside and out and, starting with the duck, place it in a suitable pan and fry in a little oil for about 5 minutes on each side. Heat the oven to the maximum and put the duck on a roasting dish and place in the oven to roast. Repeat the same procedure with the pheasants and add to the duck in the oven. Repeat again with the woodpigeon or grouse but reduce the frying time to 4 minutes each side. Repeat with the partridges, reducing the frying time to 3 minutes each side, and finally fry the quails for 2 minutes each side and add to the roast. All the birds are now in the oven at maximum temperature and should be turned and basted from time to time while you prepare the sauce.

Clean the livers from all the birds by removing all the skin and nerves, and then chop them finely. To the remaining oil and juices from the birds now add a quarter of the butter, the onion, the garlic and the livers. Fry for 10 minutes on a moderate heat, remove and set aside. In the same pan put the rest of the butter and the frozen mushrooms, increase the heat and stir-fry until you see that the mushrooms are defrosting. (If you have had the foresight to preserve mushrooms already cooked in butter then you won't need to add the extra butter.) Add the rosemary, the sage and the chives, salt, pepper and nutmeg and cook for 15 minutes; add the livers to the mushrooms and test for salt and pepper.

Meanwhile, the birds which have been roasting in the oven should now be cooked and crispy.

Start arranging the birds on the serving dish by placing the four pheasants in the middle, end to end to form a square; place the duck on top in the centre of them, arrange the woodpigeons in a circle around the pheasants, arrange the partridges in a circle around the woodpigeon, and form the outer circle with the quail. Just before serving pour the sauce over the whole dish, then serve with small Crostoni di polenta and some freshly boiled Jerusalem artichokes.

# DESSERTS

I have spent some time wondering how it might be possible to prepare mushrooms as a dessert – one might, perhaps, sweeten some slices of giant puffball with honey and then bake them. For the time being I'll wait to be convinced on desserts made from mushrooms – with the exception of the bewitching idea of my friend Gennaro which is outlined in the final recipe.

What sometimes happens on a mushroom hunt, especially when you haven't been too lucky in your hoped-for harvest, is that your attention wanders upwards towards the trees and bushes laden with those wonderful nuts and berries that can be turned into wines, syrups, jams, jellies and extremely tasty tarts. Gathering these can go a long way towards compensating for mycological disappointment, and with various of these ingredients you can create a fitting dessert for the meal in which you cook and eat the day's mushroom finds.

The subject of mushroom desserts brings to mind the cake my wife Priscilla commissioned to celebrate my fiftieth birthday. The creator was Barbara Swiderska, a former student at the Royal College of Art. She had been briefed on my mycological leanings, and came up with something that surpassed my wildest fantasies. Decorating the 4kg/8 lb iced fruit cake was a mushroom-hunter's dream – fifty wild mushrooms modelled in marzipan. They were exact replicas of real mushrooms, so perfect in size, shape and colour that it was impossible to tell them from the real thing. No doubt Barbara Swiderska had some mycological training in her native Poland. Polish people take their mushrooms very seriously – even, it seems, when these are made of marzipan.

It was two months before I could bring myself to cut such a beautiful object (fortunately it consisted of long-lasting fruit cake protected by its covering of marzipan and sugar), and during that time the 'mushrooms' fooled more than one customer at my restaurant. When the cake was cut at last it was so good that we just ate and ate and ate.

## BLUEBERRY TART

### Crostata di mirtilli

Places where mushrooms grow can also be good places for berries to grow. More than once I've returned from an Italian mushroom hunt with a punnet full of wild strawberries. On other occasions I have gathered plenty of blueberries or blackberries. They are all delicious for this tart.

*Serves 6–8*

| FOR THE PASTRY |
| --- |
| 250g/9oz/2¼ US cups flour |
| 50g/scant 2oz/¼ US cup sugar |
| a pinch of salt |
| 100g/4oz/1½ US cups unsalted butter |
| 4 tbsp dry sherry |
| FOR THE FILLING |
| 700g/1½ lb fresh blueberries |
| 150g/5oz/⅔ US cup sugar |
| the juice of half a lemon |
| 3 tbsp water |
| 4 leaves of gelatine (or the equivalent amount of powdered gelatine) |

To make the pastry, sieve together the flour, sugar and salt, add the butter cut into small pieces and mix together with your fingertips until the mixture forms crumbs. Add the sherry and mix lightly to make the dough. Cover and put aside in a cool place for at least an hour. Preheat the oven to 175°C/350°F/Gas Mark 4. Roll out the pastry and line a tart tin 25cm/10in in diameter. Prick the surface and bake blind for 15–20 minutes or until the pastry is cooked.

Meanwhile take about a third of the berries and put them in a pan together with the sugar, the lemon juice and the water. Bring to the boil and boil until the juice takes on some colour and becomes slightly syrupy. Remove from the heat, stir in the gelatine and leave to cool a little. When the pastry and the syrup have cooled, spread half the jellied syrup in a layer over the bottom of the flan. Arrange the remaining berries in a decorative way – you can make concentric circles with larger ones such as strawberries. Glaze with the remaining jellied syrup. Leave the tart to set and cool completely before serving.

## WILD HAZELNUT CAKE

### Torta con nocciole selvatiche

Hazelnut trees produce not only material for my walking sticks, but very tasty little nuts which are perfect for this cake.

*Serves 6–8*

| |
| --- |
| 125g/4½oz hazelnuts (shelled weight) |
| 100g/scant 4oz/½ US cup butter |
| 2 tsp grated lemon rind |
| 125g/4½oz/½ US cup plus 2 tbsp granulated sugar |
| 4 large eggs, separated |
| 25g/1oz/3½ tbsp flour, sifted |
| 125g/4½oz ricotta cheese |
| 6 tbsp peach or apricot jam mixed with 1 tbsp water |
| 25g/1oz bitter chocolate, grated fine |

Preheat the oven to 200°C/400°F/Gas Mark 6. Lay the hazelnuts on a metal tray and roast them for 10 minutes in the oven – they should become a light golden colour and their skins should loosen. Let them cool, then skin them (if you shake them in a sieve, most of the skins will come off). Chop the nuts finely.

Butter a 25cm/10in flan tin. Grate the rind of the lemon. Soften the butter and beat it well with 70g/3oz/⅓ US cup of the sugar, add the egg yolks and continue to beat: the mixture should be soft and foamy. Fold in the sifted flour. In a separate bowl beat the ricotta with a fork until it is light, then add the chopped hazelnuts and the grated lemon peel.

Add this mixture to the egg yolk mixture. Beat the egg whites until they become stiff, and fold in the remaining sugar. Very carefully fold the ricotta and flour mixture into the beaten egg whites.

Spread this mixture into the flan tin and bake in the oven for half an hour. Let the cake cool a little, then remove from the tin and place upside down on a plate. Dilute the jam with a little water and spread evenly over the top of the cake. Finely grate the bitter chocolate over the jam surface so that you have a light sprinkling all over. Serve with a glass of Passito di Caluso or any other good dessert wine.

## MARRONS GLACÉS

### Marrons glacés

You need to exercise a great deal of patience in order to produce the famous marrons glacés, among the sweetest and richest 'sins' ever! Half your patience will be needed to make sure that the chestnuts don't break in the cooking and peeling process, the other half to wait until they are ready to eat – and believe me, the second half is the most testing. This recipe was given to me by my sister-in-law Rosalba, who is extremely versatile in the culinary arts in her own right. She assures me that you always need to use double the quantities in order to produce the amount planned, because so many are eaten during their preparation – one or two now and then to taste for flavour; more disappear if friends call unexpectedly and have a 'taste', and many more are broken, so that from the initial number only a few remain intact and preservable. This is also one of the reasons why marrons glacés are rather expensive.

*As many as you can leave!*

| |
|---|
| 2kg/4 lb large chestnuts |
| a few bay leaves |
| a pinch of salt |
| 1kg/2 lb sugar |
| 1 cinnamon stick |
| 1 vanilla pod |

Cook the chestnuts by boiling them whole for 20–30 minutes with the bay leaves and salt: there is no need to slit the shells, because they won't explode while being boiled. Taste one to check that it is soft. (Interestingly you will receive a small dish of chestnuts cooked like this on the second day of November if you order a glass of wine in a small trattoria.)

Shell the chestnuts, using a pointed knife to remove the inner skin. Now dissolve the sugar in a pan with just a little water over a low heat, allowing it to liquefy completely; add the cinnamon and vanilla and raise the heat to medium. Place the sugar mixture in a shallow ovenproof container and add the chestnuts. Cook in a *very* low oven for 5–6 hours. At the end of this time, gently lift the chestnuts from the liquid sugar and place them on a rack to dry. They should look almost transparent and should not be sticky. Allow them to cool properly before placing them in an airtight jar to keep for as long as you can resist them.

## GENOESE CHESTNUT CAKE

### Castagnaccio Genovese

Chestnut collecting was another activity that used to lure us up into the hills in October and November, combining the joy of the atavistic hunter-gatherer with the feeling of doing something good for the family. (We sometimes found mushrooms on these occasions, but they were a bonus.) At home, we children used to roast some of the chestnuts we had collected over the fire, turning the occasion into a happy little party, or my mother would roast them in the oven. We always remembered to cut a slit in the tough shells to prevent explosions during cooking.

In northern Italy, and especially in Piedmont, chestnuts provide numerous small companies with the raw material for all sorts of goodies. Chestnuts are dried for later use, made into marrons glacés and jams, or turned into flour for the production of the famous Castagnaccio of Genoa or of Tuscany.

*Serves 6–8*

| |
|---|
| 500g/1 lb chestnut flour (obtainable from leading Italian delicatessens – it is difficult to make your own) |
| pinch of salt |
| 1 tsp fennel seeds |
| 80g/3oz raisins, soaked in a little warm water |
| 60g/2oz pine kernels |
| ½ tsp powdered cinnamon (optional) |
| 2 tbsp olive oil |
| castor sugar for sprinkling (optional) |

Preheat the oven to fairly hot – 200°C/400°F/Gas Mark 6. Put the flour into a bowl with the salt and the fennel seeds, and mix to a soft dough with some lukewarm water (use the water in which you soaked the raisins). Add the raisins, pine kernels and finally the cinnamon and mix well. Thoroughly butter a baking tin and spread the mixture on it, dribbling olive oil over the top. Place in a fairly hot oven until a golden crust has formed – about 20 minutes. The natural sweetness of the chestnuts makes additional sugar unnecessary, but when cooked you can sprinkle on a little castor sugar if you wish.

*OVERLEAF BLUEBERRY TART AND WILD HAZELNUT CAKE*

## MONT BLANC

### Monte bianco

Another famous dessert made with chestnuts is the Mont Blanc. Although marrons glacés came originally from France, the Monte Bianco pudding is very much an Italian dish because it is named after the Italian half of that famous mountain! It is rather delicious and, as you can imagine, quite rich.

| *Serves 6 or 8* |
| --- |
| 1.2kg/2½ lb large fresh chestnuts |
| enough milk to cover them |
| 1 vanilla pod |
| the peel from 1 tangerine |
| a small glass of dark rum |
| 300g/10oz icing/confectioners' sugar |
| 300ml/½ pt/1¼ US cups double (heavy) cream |
| some candied rose petals for decoration |

Peel the chestnuts and place them in boiling water for 2 minutes so that you can easily remove the inner skin with a pointed knife. (You may find it easier to work in smaller batches.) Place the chestnuts in a pan, cover with milk, add the vanilla pod and the tangerine peel and cook until soft. Remove the vanilla pod and the peel and discard them. Reduce the chestnuts to a very fine pulp, add the sugar and the rum, mix well and form the mixture into a sort of pointed mountain shape. Beat the cream almost stiff and 'snow' the mountain with it. Finally, decorate with the candied rose petals and serve. A good dessert wine, Asti Spumante perhaps, would be ideal for this pudding.

If you make the chestnut mixture a little stiffer, you could fashion a large boletus-type mushroom out of it, and the cream on top could be dotted with red sugar balls to imitate a well-known toadstool.

## ELDERBERRY CONCOCTION

### Sciroppo di sambuco

The elder is common in woods and hedges and provides precious ingredients for many wonderful things – apart from the fact that on older specimens of this tree, a delicious mushroom (not included in this book) called *Auricularia auricula-judae* (Juda's ear) can sometimes be found. White wine and champagne can be made from the flowers and red wine from the berries. I tried some elderflower champagne made by my stepson Ben and it was delicious, and I use a heavily concentrated elderflower syrup to flavour 'fools', especially those of gooseberries. In Germany I learnt how to make a vitamin-rich syrup with the ripe berries; it was reputed to be the 'toccasana' for all the winter snuffles, and it kept its promise. Every year I concoct a few jars. When diluted with hot water at the right time, the syrup produces the desired soothing effect.

| *Makes a few jars* |
| --- |
| 1½kg/3 lb full, ripe and healthy elderberries (weight without stalks) |
| 1kg/2 lb preserving sugar |
| the rind of a lemon |
| 1 cinnamon stick |
| 10 cloves |
| 1 glass of rum |

Put the berries, sugar, lemon rind, cinnamon and cloves in a stainless steel pan and place on a moderate heat. Stir from time to time until you see that everything is liquefying. Simmer for 1 hour, leave to cool and then discard the cinnamon, the lemon peel, and (if you can) the cloves. Add the rum. (You can strain the liquid if you prefer.) Put into sterilized jam jars and seal airtight. When required take 1 tablespoonful and dilute in hot water. Buona Salute.

## BEWITCHED MUSHROOMS

### Funghi stregati

Here is the delicious formula for serving mushrooms as a dessert invented by my good friend Gennaro. It consists of first blanching carefully selected mushrooms in vermouth and then preserving them in a suitable liqueur. This enables the mushrooms to be kept for some considerable time, but because they are so delicious and the temptation to eat them is so great, we have never been able to keep them for long enough to find out how long. Since the mushrooms in their liqueur are very rich, they are best used to garnish desserts such as ice cream, crème caramel and crème brûlée.

Many hours' time (and a few hangovers) have been incurred in experimenting on this recipe –

choosing mushrooms for colour, shape, texture, aroma and inherent flavour, and then matching them with a complementary liqueur. For instance, the small *Laccaria laccata* and the pretty *L. amethystea* are wonderful preserved in the Italian liqueur Strega (the name means 'witch' in English); *Craterellus infundibuliformis* is delicious in Cointreau; small *Cantharellus cibarius* (chanterelles), with their delicate apricot aroma, and *Marasmius oreades* (the fairy ring champignon) are excellent in a Hungarian apricot liqueur called Baracs; while the powerful flavour and aroma of *Clitocybe odora* (the aniseed mushroom) is ideal combined with Sambuca.

These combinations have been tried and tested, and the possibilities for further experimentation are endless – but always remember to check your mushroom identification book for any species which has an adverse effect when combined with alcohol.

| |
|---|
| 500g/1 lb small firm mushrooms |
| 1 × 75cl bottle sweet white vermouth |
| 1 small cinnamon stick |
| 4–6 cloves |
| enough liqueur to cover the mushrooms in the jar |

Clean the mushrooms very thoroughly, leaving some of the stem. Put the vermouth in a stainless steel pan and bring to the boil (take great care at this stage – boiling vermouth is inflammable), add the spices and the mushrooms and cook for 3–4 minutes. Strain and discard the spices. Allow the mushrooms to cool completely, place them in a clean jar and cover them with the liqueur. Keep the jar in the refrigerator for a while before serving.

You are sure to be bewitched by this Hansel-and-Gretel recipe.

## WILD HAZELNUT CRUNCH

### Croccante di nocciole

Almost every Christmas, I make these sweets and put them into little individual cellophane bags to give as presents to friends and relations. I make them a couple of weeks before Christmas and store them in an airtight jar to keep them crisp. A little care is needed when cooking them, as the liquid sugar used to make the hazelnuts stick together is extremely hot and can burn: I use a half-lemon as a shaping tool to save my fingers.

| *To make 1 kg of crunch* |
|---|
| 700g/1½ lb hazelnuts, shelled |
| thinly pared rind of half a lemon and half an orange |
| 700g/1½ lb sugar |
| 6 tbsp good-quality honey |
| about 10 sheets of rice paper |
| half a lemon |

Preheat the oven to 230°C/450°F/Gas Mark 8 to skin and roast the nuts. Put the hazelnuts in a metal tray and roast in the oven for about 5–10 minutes until the skins remove easily and the hazelnuts remain pale in colour. If you then shake the roasted nuts in a sieve, most of the skins will come off.

Slice the lemon and orange rind into fine strips, and then into cubes. Put the sugar in a heavy-bottomed pan along with the honey on a medium to strong flame. Stirring most of the time, cook until the sugar and honey have become liquid and turn brown in colour: this takes about 10 minutes. At this point add the rind and nuts to the caramel in the pan. Stir, keeping the pan on the heat until all the nuts are well coated. Remove from the heat.

Now lay out the sheets of rice paper and make little heaps of the hazelnut caramel using 3–4 tablespoonsful for each heap. The nuts tend to stick up from the caramel: wait till you reach the bottom of the pan and use the remaining caramel to fill up any gaps around the nuts. Flatten the heaps by patting down with the half-lemon – take care, as they will still be very hot. Leave to cool a bit, but when still warm, cut with a large knife into 2 × 3cm/1 × 1½in pieces: if the caramel is cold the knife will shatter rather than cut the pieces. Store in airtight jars.

## WALNUT LIQUEUR

### Liquore nocino

I can think of no better recipe than this, as a fitting end to this book. It is a recipe from my 'inexhaustible' Aunt Dora, or rather her own version of a famous liqueur made with wild (more or less) green walnuts. Having been made during the summer months, this reappears at Christmas time to assist, in the most pleasant way possible, the digestion of the Christmas fare.

I understand that walnut trees growing on common land are laid siege to by people wishing to pick the green walnuts at just the right time, because the curiosity of this liqueur lies in the fact that you need to pick the walnuts before the nut itself has actually formed and when the stalk and the inside are pale green and soft. This operation must be completed, according to my aunt, by 24th June – don't ask me why!

Assuming you live in a country not only where there are small walnuts already formed on the trees by 24th June, but where the alcohol in which they are to steep can be legally obtained – then you can proceed with the rest of the operation as follows:

*Makes about 2 litres/4pt of liqueur*

| |
|---|
| 16 green walnuts, cut into quarters |
| 1 litre/2pt pure edible alcohol (90°) |
| 1 tsp grated nutmeg |
| 1 tsp cloves |
| ½ litre/1pt water |
| 500g/1 lb/2 US cups castor sugar |

Place the walnuts, nutmeg, cloves and the alcohol in a glass container, and leave closed to marinate, possibly in a sunny place, for 40 days. After this time the alcohol will have assumed a very dark brown to black colour. You then add the water and the sugar, which has to be dissolved before you strain everything. Keep the liqueur in bottles. Serve in very small glasses after an opulent meal, and drink a little whenever you feel a bit down.

# A NOTE ON WINES

I am often asked whether it is prudent to drink wine with wild mushrooms, and if so, what kind. The question is not that misplaced because a few mushrooms – one is *Coprinus atramentarius* (common ink cap) – contain substances that are incompatible with alcohol; the result of consuming them together would certainly be an upset stomach, but is rarely serious.

Since wild mushrooms are difficult to digest, first of all, I would avoid eating too many at one sitting; secondly I would not drink a lot of wine with them. This doesn't mean to say that you can't enjoy a good glass of wine with mushrooms.

Italian wines are becoming better and better. Special laws have been introduced to ensure that the quality stated on the label is a true representation of the contents. It is not too difficult to find an appropriate wine to complement every dish.

A good 'rule of thumb' is to be guided by the spiciness of the food. The more delicate and subtle dishes require a very light, crisp white wine. Included in this category I would recommend Blanc de Morgex from the Aosta valley; and Erbaluce di Caluso, Cortese and Gavi, all from Piedmont. From north-east Italy come delicate wines such as Soave, Pino Grigio, Colli Enganei Bianco and Pinot Bianco. Albana di Romagna represents the region with the richest food. Vermentino from Liguria is quite delicate. Tuscany and Sardinia offer Vernaccia, of which that from S. Gimignano is the more delicate. Orvieto from Umbria, Colli Albani and Frascati from Lazio, and Verdicchio from Marche are other light and crispy wines. In Sicily I discovered a wine called Donna Fugata Bianco that is most suitable for delicate mushrooms. Really delicious!

Rosés and light reds are the wines most suitable for tastier dishes where the flavour of the mushrooms or other ingredients are more distinctive, though some of the more full-bodied whites are also a good choice.

Piemontesi drink either a good Dolcetto, Grignolino or Barbaresco to accompany their strongly flavoured dishes based on white truffles: personally, I wouldn't mind having a glass of a strong, dry spumante of a good vintage with truffles. Chiaretto of the Riviera del Garda, and various Trameno or Santa Maddalena or Caldaro are the cool, light representatives of Alto Adige. Tocai is quite a strong white wine which goes well with strongly flavoured dishes.

Sangiovese di Romagna and very young Chianti wines from Tuscany compete with a powerful white wine from Campania called Falerno as suitable candidates for drinking with powerful dishes.

There is a strong rosé wine from Puglia called Five Roses which I would drink with the most strongly flavoured dishes based on wild mushrooms and game. Those dishes could also be accompanied by Barolo from Piedmont, or Brunello di Montalcino and Vino Nobile di Montepulciano from Tuscany. Interesting strong wines from other regions are Carema and Nebbiolo from Piedmont, Grumello and Sassella from Lombardy, Recioto Amarone from Veneto, Taurasi from Campania, Rosso di Cerignola from Puglia, and finally, Cirò di Calabria and Donna Fugata Rosso from Sicily.

# PRESERVING MUSHROOMS

The art of preserving food is as old as the history of humanity itself. Prehistoric hunters who caught a large animal were confronted with the same problem that we face today when we are lucky enough to collect a great quantity of mushrooms: what shall we do with them all? How can we keep some? One prehistoric solution to prolonging the bonanza of a large steak was to hang strips of meat outside the cave to dry in the air and a later one was to pack them in salt, and these methods are paralleled in the traditional techniques of drying and salting mushrooms. Later, pickling and bottling or canning offered additional ways of preserving mushrooms, and most recently freezing has opened up new possibilities. Different mushrooms call for different approaches. The various methods maintain, enhance or even transform the natural qualities of the original, and your choice depends both on the means you have available and on how you want to use your preserves.

Speaking personally, no matter which way I preserve mushrooms, I always enjoy them and continually find new ways of using them. From the anonymity of the convenient frozen blocks of mushrooms in the freezer to the rows of glass jars packed with dried and pickled delights which turn my larder into a mycophagist's Aladdin's cave, preserving enables me to serve wild mushrooms all the year round. And perhaps at Christmas, you, like me, will be able to give your friends presents made up of a small bottle of mushroom extract together with a little bag of dried mushrooms, and pretty jars packed with pickles.

## DRYING

Until a couple of years ago anyone entering our house in autumn was assaulted by an intense smell of wild mushrooms, and confronted in every room – the studio, the spare bedrooms and wherever else I could find space – by sheets of newspaper spread with thin slices of drying *Boletus edulis* and *B. badius*. In Italy a similar ritual is followed religiously, though there the hot sun means the mushrooms can be spread outside and the whole procedure takes only a day. Then, in Switzerland, I came across a machine purpose-built for drying mushrooms. It consists of a fan which blows warm air from a round base which supports several wire baskets arranged in tiers. Now, using up to seven baskets at a time, I can completely dry 3kg/6½lb mushrooms in about two hours. An extra advantage is that this machine enables me to dry mushrooms such as *Lepista nuda* that are generally considered too moist.

Ideally, drying captures and preserves the taste, aroma and texture of mushrooms so that they can be enjoyed out of season. Very few mushrooms retain their shape after they have been reconstituted by soaking in water – morels, *Sparassis crispa* and shiitake are exceptions. Others lose their physical characteristics but retain what is most important – the taste and aroma. Dried mushrooms are extremely versatile in any type of cuisine: just one or two pieces or a sprinkling of powder will enhance the flavour of a dish.

### Mushrooms to dry
Not all mushrooms are suitable: the fibrous texture makes some stringy and tough, while others lose their aroma. The best results come from:
*Boletus edulis* (cep): This not only has the perfect fleshy texture for slicing and drying, but actually intensifies in taste when dried, and reconstitutes reasonably well. Italy has a long-established industry dedicated to preparing and selling dried *porcini* – the best of all are said to come from Val di Borgataro. Considering the price of the fresh mushrooms, and that they lose up to 90 per cent of their weight in drying, it is no wonder that just a little amount is expensive. If you dry your own or buy those imported from elsewhere you will find them less flavoursome than the Italian ones, but still worth while.
*Boletus badius* (bay bolete): Although the flavour is less intense than that of the cep, the texture is similar and it dries equally well. Since it is a common mushroom, I dry large quantities and find it very useful.

*Morchella elata* and *M. esculenta* (morels): Probably the most expensive to buy dried, since they are much sought after and have a short season in spring. High gastronomy – especially French and Swiss cuisines – makes abundant use of morels, fresh and dried. Dried morels reconstitute well, with a good taste and texture in my opinion, but relatively little aroma. They can be dried whole. Look out for dirt at the stem base in bought ones.
*Craterellus cornucopioides* (horn of plenty): Ideal for drying because of the absence of watery flesh and the increase in aroma when dry. It reconstitutes well, and is also extremely easy to reduce to powder.
*Sparassis crispa* (cauliflower fungus): Ideal for drying because of its good texture and slight aroma: when reconstituted, it assumes the same cartilaginous quality it has when fresh, and so is perfect for soups and other dishes requiring a little texture. I have even managed to coat the revived dried version in egg and breadcrumbs and deep-fried it successfully. Cut in slices for drying.

Suitable but not so highly recommended are *Agaricus campestris* (field mushroom), *Armillaria mellea* (honey fungus), *Hydnum repandum* (hedgehog fungus) and *Suillus grevillei* (larch bolete). Least successful of all is *Cantharellus cibarius* (chanterelle), which becomes tough and fairly tasteless when dried – the only thing it retains is its charming colour.

### Hints
Never wash mushrooms to be dried: brush or cut away parts such as the base of the stem that are dirty or sandy (residual particles of sand will fall away when the mushrooms are dry).

Use only fresh specimens that are mature, not overripe. The odd insect larva in a large cep doesn't matter – it will vacate its habitat once the mushroom is sliced.

Smallish mushrooms can be threaded whole on to string (allowing space for the air to circulate between them) and hung up to dry. They can be rethreaded for storage. Otherwise, cut cap and stem of larger fleshy mushrooms such as boletes into slices 5mm/¼in thick.

In warm climates, lay the mushroom slices on gauze-covered mats and place in the sun – they should dry in a day. In colder and more humid regions, it is safer to dry them indoors. Spread them on a layer of clean newspaper covered by a clean cloth, and leave in a well-ventilated room, turning the mushrooms from time to time to ensure thorough drying. The top of a central-heating radiator and an airing cupboard with good air circulation are also suitable places. Mushrooms can be dried in a fan oven – set at a *very* low temperature, or they will cook – with the door slightly open. Whichever method you choose, dry the mushrooms as quickly as possible.

Store mushrooms in airtight jars or polythene bags – but *only* when they are perfectly dry, otherwise they will go mouldy.

*Mushroom powder* can be made from completely dry mushrooms using a pestle and mortar or a food processor. Keep in an airtight jar and add to soups and sauces, or incorporate in savoury butters and fresh pasta dough. Dried *Boletus edulis*, *B. badius* and *Craterellus cornucopioides* are perhaps best for this purpose, but other kinds can be added to obtain a good mixture.

### Buying dried mushrooms
Inspect mushrooms that claim to be best quality to make sure they contain whole slices (minus maggot holes) and that you are not paying for scrappy bits. Inferior grades are usually sold cheaper, and contain more oddments.

### Reconstituting dried mushrooms
Soak in lukewarm water: the average time is 15 minutes or so, before cooking as directed in the recipe. Dried shiitake will take longer – 30 minutes; discard the stem, which is usually tough and dirty. Use the soaking water – filtered to remove any grit from the mushrooms – for flavour in the same recipe or in stock. (Alternatively, the slow cooking process of soups and some sauces may be enough to revive the mushrooms in itself, and they can be added dried.)

## SALTING

With drying, salting must be one of the oldest ways of preserving food. It is still widely used in Poland and Russia not only for meat and fish but also for vegetables – including mushrooms. The process simply consists of burying the mushrooms in plenty of salt, which gradually dissolves into a preservative brine. *Lactarius deliciosus* is one kind traditionally salted, but any young firm mushrooms are ideal candidates for this treatment.

Once you have cleaned the mushrooms thoroughly (without, of course, washing them) – removing any grit, checking for maggots, etc – you alternate layers of sea or rock salt and layers of mushrooms in non-corrosive containers such as earthenware crocks or glass jars. Allow approximately 1 part salt to 3 parts mushrooms by weight. Begin and end with a layer of salt. You can add more mushrooms and salt in the same way, filling the jar as you find them. Press the contents down well and cover closely.

When you want to use some, rinse well and cook without additional salt. Watch the seasoning of soups and stews – these mushrooms will salt the dish for you sufficiently.

## FREEZING

Since they may be up to 90 per cent water, mushrooms are not difficult to freeze; the problem arises when you come to thaw them and want something resembling a mushroom rather than an indefinable mess. Experiments have shown me which mushrooms have a structure that enables them to be frozen raw without becoming tough or 'frostbitten' and which ones need blanching before freezing, and I have also evolved reliable ways of defrosting them. Most mushrooms can be frozen after some preliminary cooking, and I include one or two recommendations on this.

### Freezing raw mushrooms
Good to freeze raw are: the *Agaricus* species (though personally I wouldn't bother with them, since the cultivated ones are available all year round); *Boletus edulis* (cep) and *B. badius* (bay bolete) – these two are the best; *Craterellus cornucopioides* (horn of plenty), *Hydnum repandum* (hedgehog fungus) and *Leccinum versipelle* (orange birch bolete). *Lactarius deliciosus* (saffron milk cap) freezes perfectly after blanching. Other mushrooms need cooking before they freeze successfully.

Choose only small and maggot-free specimens. Clean thoroughly, put 8 or 10 at a time in a transparent plastic bag and seal, extracting as much air as possible. Put in the deep freeze and keep frozen at a maximum of −18°C/0°F. Or open-freeze the mushrooms on a tray and then bag them. Remember to date and label the bags.

Defrost either by my special method of dropping the frozen mushrooms into a deep-frier for a few seconds – the frying seals the outside and defrosts the inside (be careful not to let the oil bubble over); or by plunging them into boiling salted water for a few minutes until they are soft, then drain, slice and use as if fresh.

### Freezing in butter
My own favourite way of freezing boletes in

particular is to cook them in butter, which helps protect them against 'frostbite'. Use plenty of butter – 250g/½ lb to every 750g/1½ lb mushrooms. Gently fry a couple of very finely chopped onions in the butter until golden, put in the sliced mushrooms and stir-fry for 10–12 minutes. Cool, then put into plastic freezer boxes with lids, labelling with the date and type of mushroom, and freeze.

To defrost, leave the block at room temperature for an hour or use a microwave. The mushrooms and butter are the ready-made basis for soups and sauces, or can be used by themselves. They are ideal for risotto, where you won't be able to tell the difference from fresh mushrooms.

### Freezing duxelles

This method is suitable for any type of mushroom, or an assortment, and since the mixture is chopped finely, you can use every edible piece. It is the standard way of beginning sauces and soups whether you freeze them or not, and produces a ready-made filling for stuffed pasta. I freeze the mixture in an ice-cube tray, removing the cubes to a plastic bag when they are solid. (The amazing advantage of doing this is that you don't have to defrost the whole block of mushrooms when you only want a little to flavour a sauce.)

| |
|---|
| 50g/2oz/4 tbsp butter |
| 2 onions, finely sliced |
| 2 or 3 grates of nutmeg |
| 1kg/2 lb mushrooms, cleaned and cut in chunks |
| salt and pepper to taste |

Put the butter in a pan, add the onion and nutmeg and fry for a few minutes. Add the mushrooms and cook until the liquid evaporates. Add salt and pepper to taste, allow to cool and chop finely in a food processor before freezing.

## PICKLING

Whether the mushrooms are to be kept in brine or in olive oil, they are first pickled in a vinegar solution. This means they lose their aromatic subtlety, but retain their texture and appearance to remind one of past summer days. And since the traditional antipasto must include something piquant and vinegary to tease the appetite, these delicacies are just what is needed. Commercially you will only find pickled *porcini* – the same industry that markets dried mushrooms is busy producing jars of pickled ones, including artistic jars of small whole ceps beautifully arranged by hand and costing a fortune – but almost all the edible mushrooms described in this book are suitable subjects for experiment: I quite like to serve a mixture.

### Pickled mushrooms in brine

This method is the more economical, but the product has to be mixed with some oil before serving to make it more palatable and to reduce the sharpness. The taste of the vinegar can be softened by adding extra herbs. Choose only the most tender specimens, because they are most likely to be maggot-free, and be sure to clean them thoroughly – for once you can use water to rinse them immediately before cooking. Mushrooms reduce in volume by about half when pickled, so calculate accordingly when filling your jars. (These should be sterilized screw-top jars, and small ones are a good idea since once opened the contents need to be consumed soon.) The following quantities are for 2kg/4 lb raw mushrooms, cleaned and sliced or cut up according to size:

| |
|---|
| 1 litre/2pt good white wine vinegar |
| 500ml/1pt water |
| 1 tbsp salt |
| small sprig of rosemary |
| few black peppercorns |
| 5–6 bay leaves |
| 1 medium onion, quartered |
| 2 cloves garlic, peeled |

Combine the ingredients and boil for 15 minutes. Meanwhile, cook the mushrooms separately in salted water for 8 minutes, drain, add to the vinegar and boil together for a further 5 minutes. Remove the mushrooms with a sterilized spoon and fill your jars with them, leaving some space for the liquor. Let the brine cook for a further 10 minutes and set aside to cool. When completely cool, cover the mushrooms with the liquor. Cover the jars: they will keep for a long time.

To serve, drain the mushrooms and toss in a few drops of olive oil.

### Pickled mushrooms in oil

This second method, the usual one in Italy, is slightly more expensive since the mushrooms have to be immersed for keeping in pure olive oil – but I can tell you that the results are so delicious that it is well worth it. As for the previous recipe, only the best tender young specimens should be used, and absolute cleanliness is paramount. Quantities for 2kg/4lb raw mushrooms, cleaned and cut up according to size:

| |
|---|
| 1 litre/2pt good white wine vinegar |
| 500ml/1pt water |
| 2 tbsp salt |
| 5 bay leaves |
| 10 cloves |

Bring the brine ingredients to the boil, add the mushrooms and boil for 5–10 minutes, depending on the kind of mushrooms. Drain the mushrooms and, without using your hands because the mushrooms are now sterilized, spread on a very clean cloth to cool and dry for a few hours. Sterilize jars that can be tightly closed. Put a few mushrooms into a jar, pour in a little olive oil to cover them and (using the same spoon for each operation) mix gently so that the oil reaches all parts of the mushrooms. Add more mushrooms and more oil in the same way until the jar is full, close the lid tightly and keep for at least a month before use. Once opened, a jar should be used up fairly rapidly.

Occasionally I find *a few* pinpoints of mould on the mushrooms after some months. If I catch this early enough the situation can be retrieved. I throw away the oil, boil the mushrooms in pure vinegar for a minute or so, then store in fresh olive oil as before.

## BOTTLING

Based on the principle used in canning food, the sterilizing or pasteurizing process kills micro-organisms by extremely thorough heating and seals the food from outside contamination. It is somehow a neutral method in the sense that it preserves food 'au naturel', without introducing alien agents or preserving agents, so that you can use it in many different ways, though the ingredients do change in consistency and lose some taste. The only way to preserve truffles, for example (though with a tremendous loss of aromatic value) is through sterilization 'al naturale'. It is also possible to preserve previously cooked food – sauces and so on – by this method.

My mother used to show me her tricks for ensuring that the sterilization process turned out perfectly: she would add quite a lot of salt to the water in which the jars were heated, increasing the water temperature by a few extra degrees. She kept the jars separate with cloth to prevent them touching and cracking during the boiling process, and allowed the jars to cool completely in the water before testing the seal and storing them. Above all, she used very fresh and impeccably clean raw material. Her mushrooms were cooked briefly in slightly salted water before being bottled.

Though the Carluccio family seemed to thrive on the food thus prepared, this method is unfortunately not good enough for today's hygiene experts, who fear the risk of botulism from bottling vegetables (including mushrooms), which are low in acidity. They advise using a pressure cooker to attain a sufficiently high temperature and recommend 40 minutes at 4.5kg/10lb pressure for mushrooms. The whole business is so complicated that I'll refer you to your cookery manual for all the technical details. In fact, I suggest you use the deep freeze instead!

## MUSHROOM EXTRACT

A useful way of coping with either a mixture of small quantities of different mushrooms or a glut of any one kind is to make this concentrate to keep in the refrigerator and use for flavouring all sorts of dishes. Clean the mushrooms, chop them finely, put them in a little water and boil until they have exuded as much as possible of their natural juices. The mushrooms themselves will be pretty tasteless, though they could go to make up a quantity for pickling; if you don't want to eat them, strain off the liquor and discard them. Add to the liquor a sprig of rosemary, some sage leaves, a few bay leaves, some pepper and a lot of salt. (I further reinforce the mushroom flavour by adding some dried mushrooms and garlic.) Boil until the liquid starts to thicken, then pour into a clean bottle and store in the refrigerator. Once you have made some you will probably not want to keep it too long – you will use a drop here and a drop there, and it will disappear in no time.

# —PART 2—
# THE FIELD GUIDE

## WHAT ARE MUSHROOMS?

As a child searching for mushrooms with a friendly guide I never asked myself what mushrooms were. All I knew was that the ones we collected were beautiful, hard to find and exceptionally good to eat. As an adult I found myself wanting to know more, and voraciously devoured all the books I could find on the subject of mycology (the scientific study of fungi – from the Greek *mykes* meaning fungus). I lay no claim now to being a fully fledged mycologist, able to tell you about all aspects of the fungus world: my main interest is in finding, cooking and eating the edible wild mushrooms, so I'm more a sort of mycophile and mycophagist – one who loves mushrooms, and likes very much to eat them. It is true that in the four decades of my obsession, I have become pretty well informed mycologically: while in pursuit of something for the pot, you can't help picking up a good deal of general mushroom lore. But I would like to stress that serious mushroom hunters should refer to a comprehensive field guide. Here I intend to give full information only about the most important edible species, as well as their poisonous lookalikes.

What we know as a mushroom is only the ephemeral fruit-body stage of the complex fungus organism as a whole. For the moment, let's concentrate on this fruit-body from the consumer's point of view.

## COLLECTING MUSHROOMS

Understanding certain aspects of mycology gives practical clues as to where and when to look, and makes sense of some of the rituals of collecting.

### Where

Many of the edible species of fungus favour specific types of habitat and have particular requirements in terms of host nutrient. This not only means that it is worth making forays in likely-looking places with the appropriate sort of vegetation, but can be a key element in identifying an unfamiliar specimen. Some fungus species grow on living or decaying wood, others on soil or dung. Certain mushrooms have a symbiotic relationship with certain plants, often trees and shrubs. Sometimes this mycorrhizal association (the Greek *rhiza* means root) is with a specific tree, sometimes with more than one. As examples, *Suillus grevillei* (the larch bolete) – as its common name suggests – prefers larch trees.

*Leccinum* mushrooms grow almost exclusively among birch. *Lactarius deliciosus* and *Suillus luteus* prefer pine trees, particularly Scots pines. *Boletus edulis* and *B. badius* grow among oak, birch, beech and pine. If you know your trees, it helps you know your mushrooms.

Morels, one of the first mushrooms to appear in spring, prefer the edges of broad-leaved woodland but will also be found under poplar and in gardens, orchards, wasteland and even burnt ground. Field mushrooms and giant puffballs are found in open fields and meadows, and are the exceptions to the rule that mushrooms prefer warm, damp, shady places. On the whole you will find most mushrooms in

humus-rich soil, in places that are not too marshy, nor overgrown with thick tall vegetation.

As you search, keep your eyes open for local clues, such as scattered caps of boletes – the leftovers from a squirrel's meal of the stems of these delicacies – which tell you to look for others growing somewhere in the vicinity. As you recognize more and more types of fungi you can use them as signposts to the edible species. Where you see the beautiful but poisonous *Amanita muscaria* (fly agaric), for example, look especially carefully: *Boletus edulis* (cep) enjoys the same environment, and is a good mushroom to start collecting. It is the easiest to recognize and tastiest of all.

A SPECIES OF OYSTER MUSHROOM, *PLEUROTUS CORNUCOPIAE*

Keep a note of your landmarks as you wander in search of mushrooms: it is easy to get disorientated. Once you have discovered a 'good' place, mark it on your map so that you can visit it again next season: since the mycelium is long-lasting, mushrooms can often be found in the same place year after year. And don't share your secret with too many friends, in case they turn into competitors.

## When

The season varies according to the individual species. A few edible mushrooms (morels among them) appear in spring, but most appear from mid- or late summer on through the autumn, and some continue after the first frosts. The right preconditions of temperature and humidity produce a flush of fruit bodies: you can expect them to appear in warm weather following rain. Given optimum conditions – moist soil and a temperature of 18–25°C/65–77°F the fruit bodies of *Boletus edulis* can deveop in four or five days, and you know roughly when it is worth returning to the same spot for the new crop – if someone else has not beaten you to it. It is for this reason that you will often find me out hunting on a

Wednesday. Mushrooming is a weekend activity for many people, and the best places are often stripped bare of mushrooms by enthusiasts. By midweek there is often a flush of new growth, and the tiny specimens of the weekend are large enough to be worth picking.

Although rain is necessary for mushrooms' development, avoid collecting them in the rain or immediately afterwards. They will have absorbed too much water and be heavy and soggy in your basket. If they are not already an unappetizing mess by the time you get them home, they will exude an excessive amount of water when you cook them.

Every year I wait for the right conditions for the mushroom season to begin with the impatience of a small child. Although I have a good 'nose' for mushrooms, I am often a few days too early and the first trip or two into the woods may not be very productive – not of mushrooms, at least: instead I often come back with some consolation prizes in the form of new walking sticks to carve and decorate. Even in the height of the season my impatience has sometimes taken me to a mushroom spot in such good time that I have had to wait in the car for an hour or so before dawn breaks.

## Picking mushrooms

For identification purposes, you need to gather the entire fruit-body, base and all, preferably with both young and mature specimens to compare development, and carry them home wrapped in waxed paper to preserve their freshness. The points to examine are summarized in the introduction to the Field Guide on page 133. Keep these unidentified specimens well away from any you are intending to eat.

Once you have learned to recognize edible species, you can go out with your basket and knife to harvest as many as you can. A basket, because it permits you to transport delicate mushrooms without crushing or breaking them and (unlike plastic) allows the air to circulate freely around them. You should never collect or keep mushrooms in a plastic bag – in warm weather they will sweat and lose condition quickly, becoming contaminated with bacteria. If you need a receptacle to take the overflow from your basket, carry a cotton bag folded in your pocket; failing that, an ordinary paper bag is a useful last resort. In mushroom-gatherers' lore, the open weave of a basket has the further advantage of allowing the spores to escape freely and be distributed along your route.

As you pile up your mushrooms in your basket, it is a good idea to do some preliminary cleaning so that grit from the upper layer of mushrooms does not fall into the gills or pores of those below. This is one of the functions of the knife: to trim away the dirty stem base and scrape off twigs or pine needles adhering to the stem or cap. A particularly sophisticated knife I found in Italy was specifically designed for mushroom gathering. Its slightly curved blade is serrated on one side to scrape earth off the mushroom stem, and it incorporates a brush to dust sand off the mushroom. The minimum sizes of mushroom you are allowed to pick in Italy are printed on one side of this knife – another piece of evidence that shows how seriously Italians take the subject.

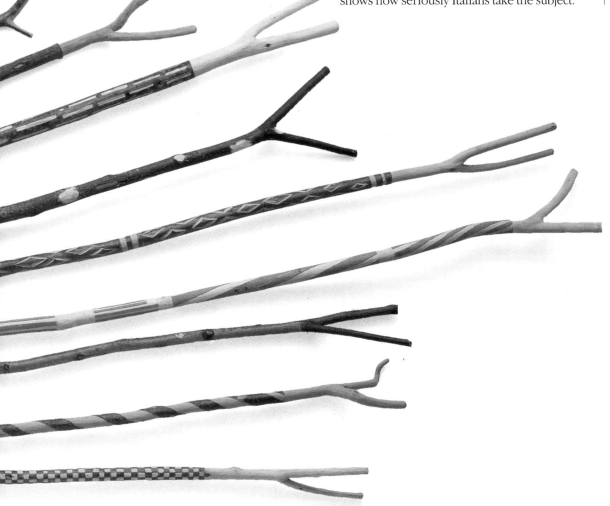

In the Field Guide you will find appropriate advice on picking and cleaning individual species – such as whether to discard the stem, to cut or twist the mushroom from the mycelium, or (in just one instance) to peel the cap. Generally, try not to disturb the mycelium too much by tearing the mushroom out of the ground.

You will develop your own list of additional equipment, from wellington boots to protect against wet grass and brambles to bars of chocolate to sustain you on your quest. Perhaps like me you will accumulate a set of useful thumbsticks to brush aside undergrowth that you think may be concealing a mushroom and (if you are in snake country) to pin down any malicious snake that may cross your path. I'm sure I do not need to remind you to respect the country code and leave the plants and animals you meet in peace, nor to tell you to keep calm even when you see a rival heading for your favourite 'patch'... Good hunting!

BOLETE DISPLAY AND BASKET BRIMMING WITH THE DAY'S HAUL

## IDENTIFYING MUSHROOMS

To identify a mushroom expertly you have to be sure of every single element: checking physical characteristics observable in the field such as shape, colour, texture and smell is part of the procedure, as well as noting the habitat itself; accurate identification can ultimately depend on examining microscopic details such as the precise form of the individual spore. Fortunately, however, the wild mushrooms with which we are concerned are those with a clearly visible (and good-tasting) fruit-body, and if you systematically check a specimen against the description of cap, stem, gills, spore colour, etc in the Field Guide below, you should go a long way towards establishing its identity. The surest safeguard is to consult a professional mycologist who will

identify specimens accurately before you eat anything: you will often find such an expert if you join fungus forays organized by local naturalist groups or professional mycological societies. (Another alternative is to marry one, as my wife Priscilla did!)

Mycological experts themselves are slow to reach any agreement about the definitive classification of certain fungi, and this is why you

will find the botanical Latin names varying from book to book (and why I have included some of the more widely used synonyms in this one). I recommend your buying two or more good books on identifying fungi (see the note on further reading on page 188). Just as it is useful to have more than one reference book to clarify the names (a giant puffball is a giant puffball whether known by the generic name *Langermannia*, *Lycoperdon* or *Calvatia*), you get a very helpful perspective on identifying a specimen by comparing both the descriptions and the illustrations in different books.

I hope you will find, as I have done, that a modest amount of basic mycology is useful to define some terms and to help you understand what you are looking for when you carry out your examination of the mushrooms in your basket.

## How a mushroom is produced

The world of fungi (which embraces mushrooms) is far, far vaster than I ever imagined. This part of the vegetable universe differs from plants in containing no chlorophyll, the green pigment by which plants synthesize carbon compounds from the sun's energy. (There is even some dispute as to whether to call fungi plants at all.) Fungi draw their nutrition from living organisms – plants, or even animals – or from decaying organic matter. Many of them play a complex ecological role: by feeding off and assimilating decaying matter they are recycling carbohydrates necessary to the equilibrium of nature, as well as performing a clearing-up job in assisting decomposition.

There are many thousands of microscopic fungi that regulate our own lives in one way or another. Some combat illness by producing well-known antibiotics such as penicillin. Some are destructive, such as the malicious *Ceratocystis ulmi*, Dutch elm disease, which is carried by certain beetles. Then again it is the action of fungi that converts sugar into alcohol during wine making, that turns milk into yoghurt and that makes bread rise.

These are micro-organisms. With the edible mushrooms, however, we are concerned with a single stage in the life cycle of the larger and more evolved 'higher fungi'. The mushroom itself is only a part of the story. Underlying this ephemerally visible part of the fungus is the more permanent mycelium. This is the important vegetative part of the mushroom and it should never be disturbed by inconsiderate collecting. Like the entire fruit body of the mushroom itself,

it is formed of a complex of many microscopic filaments called hyphae. Hyphae are produced by the spores on germination as a branching thread which spreads in the soil or leaf litter forming a sort of web and often travelling for several metres absorbing suitable substances to support the growth of the fungus.

When climatic conditions such as moisture and temperature are appropriate, the organism reproduces by rapidly developing a fruit-body. The spores, produced in millions by each single mushroom when it reaches full maturity, are discharged from the hymenium (the fertile spore-producing surface) to be dispersed by the wind or in other ways. On landing upon the ground in favourable conditions they will germinate and form a new mycelium.

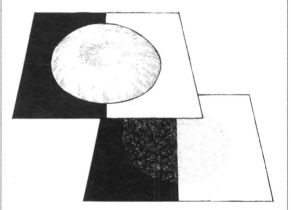

*Spore prints* Spores are microscopic and vary in shape and colour from mushroom to mushroom. Even without a microscope it is possible to see the colour of the spores en masse: all you have to do is leave the cap of a mushroom on glass or paper for a few hours. The spores will drop out leaving a 'print' clearly visible to the naked eye. (It is always a good idea to use a piece of paper that is half white and half black so the print is clearly visible whether the spores are light or dark.) Like a fingerprint, the information contained in the spore is essential for correct identification. Although the shape of the spore itself can be seen only under a microscope, the colour of the 'print', plus all the other field characteristics, will help you name the mushroom you have collected.

## The main mushroom groups

Mycologists divide the larger fungi into two major groups – Ascomycetes and Basidiomycetes – according to the way they produce spores. Ascomycetes, the 'spore-shooters', which develop spores internally within a sac called an ascus from which they are violently discharged at maturity,

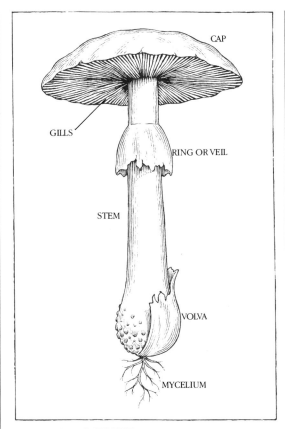

PARTS OF THE AGARIC TYPE

comprise a diverse range of often bizarrely shaped fruit-bodies, including cup fungi. I have included only two ascomycetes in my selection for the mycophagist, but since these consist of the highly prized morel and the almost mythical truffle, their gastronomic importance outweighs their numerical insignificance.

The second group, the Basidiomycetes, covers the rest of the edible mushrooms in this book. Among them are two well-known categories of conventionally mushroom-shaped mushrooms, with more or less convex caps and central stems.

**Agarics – gill fungi –** have radiating gills on the underside of the fleshy cap. The spores are produced on the hymenium, which covers the gill surface. It is vital to study the colour and the mode of attachment of the gills to identify agarics correctly [see diagram]. Some fungi in this group also have a volva – an egg-shaped membrane which encloses the small developing mushroom, and which ruptures as the developing mushroom grows. Sometimes part of the volva remains on top of the cap of the mature mushroom in the form of flakes or scales. Another characteristic of many agarics is the veil – the membrane that in young specimens encloses and protects the gills but which, as the young fruit-body expands, is ruptured to leave a sort of skirt or ring round the stem. The gilled category of mushrooms is extremely large and includes such familiar genera as *Agaricus, Amanita, Armillaria, Cantharellus, Clitocybe, Cortinarius, Laccaria, Lactarius, Lepiota, Lepista, Pleurotus, Russula* and *Tricholoma*.

**Boletes – pore fungi –** have a fruit-body which is fleshy, convex and centrally stalked; the lower surface of the cap has a poroid sponge-like appearance. The pores differ in their density and colour from bolete to bolete. When young they tend to be cream in colour, turning to yellowish/greenish later – but are of a reddish tone in some species. Bruising the pores also gives an indication of the type, especially if the colour changes to blue or to black. This group includes the genera *Boletus, Gyroporus, Leccinum, Suillus* and *Tylopilus*.

Other edible Basidiomycetes are a more motley crew. Hedgehog fungi have the hymenium covering spikes or spines which hang from the underside of the cap. (*Hydnum repandum* could be confused with a pale pinkish mushroom or bolete from above, until one sees the spiny lower surface.) Bracket fungi, like boletes, have a poroid hymenium, but differ from boletes in their woody and leathery texture, their usually fan-shaped or shell-shaped brackets and their occurrence on wood. *Fistulina hepatica* and *Laetiporus sulphureus* are edible examples. *Sparassis crispa* is in a category of its own. Puffballs, gasteromycetes which 'puff' out their spores when hit by raindrops, are also Basidiomycetes.

PARTS OF THE BOLETE TYPE

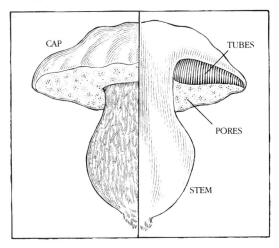

# AGARICUS CAMPESTRIS

(syn PSALLIOTA CAMPESTRIS)

### Field Mushroom (UK)/Meadow Mushroom (USA)

F: rose des prés   G: Wiesenchampignon   I: prataiolo
P: pieczarka polna   Sp: champiñon

I am happy that there is at least one type of wild mushroom that a lot of people recognize and enjoy picking and eating with safety. The field mushroom (*Agaricus campestris*) and its larger cousin, the horse mushroom (*A. arvensis* syn *Psalliota arvensis*), can be found fairly extensively in their preferred habitat of well-manured pastures, when the summer weather has been wet and warm. Both mushrooms are related to *Agaricus bisporus*, the commercially cultivated 'champignon' one finds in every supermarket and greengrocers.

Often when I talk to someone about my passion for mushrooms, I am amused to hear them say, 'Oh yes, I know *mushrooms* ...' meaning field mushrooms, and implying that everything else is a toadstool. One thing that worries me in this blithe assurance is the possibility of a non-expert mistakenly collecting the poisonous 'yellow stainer' (*Agaricus xanthodermus*) which can be found in the same fields and meadows, as well as in gardens and shrubberies. So when you find a colony of what looks like field mushrooms, avoid picking those that have yellow stains on their stems or caps, especially if these stains are at the base of the stem, and become a deeper chrome yellow when bruised. Above all, avoid any look-alikes which have *white* gills: they could be the deadly-poisonous *Amanita verna* or *A. virosa*.

## RECOGNITION

### Agaricus campestris

**Cap** round at first, very tightly attached to stem; becoming convex and expanding to 10cm/4in diameter. White, becoming cream/brown.
**Gills** adnexed, pale pink at first deepening to dark brown when fully grown. Spore print: purple-brown.
**Stem** relatively thick and short (1–2cm/⅜–¾in diameter and 3–8cm/1¼–3in tall), with slight frill-like ring.
**Flesh** white, bruising slightly pink. Taste and smell pleasant and mushroomy.
**Habitat** pastureland, especially when richly manured; occasionally in gardens or park edges. Field mushrooms usually grow scattered or in clusters, but occasionally you find them in rings.
**Season** early summer to late autumn, especially when wet and warm.

### Agaricus arvensis

The principal difference is in size: the horse mushroom is generally larger and more substantial, the cap growing to 20cm/8in diameter and the stem to 10cm/4in tall, with a distinctive cog-wheel-like ring. The caps of the bigger horse mushrooms are very fleshy and heavy, but the stems tend to become hollow. The flesh smells pleasantly of aniseed. While field

mushrooms are generally maggot-free, larger horse mushrooms tend to become infested.

## CLEANING AND COOKING

As these mushrooms are widely considered to be *the* only edible kind, it is not surprising to find them used in recipes throughout the world. They can be eaten raw in salads (especially the smaller firmer young specimens), cooked in stews and soups and served with almost every type of food. Excellent deep-fried or reduced to duxelles. They can be pickled and preserved to serve as antipasti. Preserving by freezing and drying are not recommended – but since the very similar commercially grown species is so readily available throughout the year, this perhaps does not matter; the wild mushrooms are somehow tastier, though.

Clean with just a wipe if necessary – there is no need to peel. The whole mushroom can be used – discard the stalks of older specimens if they are no longer fleshy and tender.

# AMANITA CAESAREA

Caesar's Mushroom

Fr: amanite impériale; oronge   G: Kaiserling   I: ovolo
P: muchomor cesarski   Sp: oronja

*Amanita caesarea* is so named, history tells us, because it was the favourite of the Roman Emperor, and the tradition lives on in the English name of 'Caesar's mushroom', the French 'impériale', the Polish 'cesarski' and the German 'Kaiserling'. The Italians, on the other hand, call it 'ovolo' because when it is very small it looks like an egg in size and colour. Even in the Mediterranean region the mushroom is fairly rare (it is found mostly in the hills of northern Italy), and because of its demand as a delicacy the price can easily reach £50 per kilo. So far this mushroom has never been found in Britain: perhaps some ardent mushroom-hunting reader can lay claim to fame by being the first to find one.

I once had a meal fit for a king in a restaurant in Milan. A salad of raw 'ovoli' with raw 'porcini' (*Boletus edulis*) – topped with some freshly sliced white Alba truffle (*Tuber magnatum*). An unforgettable dish for a mycophagist!

It is quite extraordinary that in the *Amanita* genus you can find both the deadliest mushrooms and this one, which is the most delicious of all. Fortunately identification is easy, and there is no danger of mistaking the edible rarity for the poisonous *Amanita phalloides* (death cap) or *A. muscaria* (fly agaric).

## RECOGNITION

**Cap** the egg-like volva splits to reveal the deep red cap; as it expands from hemispherical to convex, the cap pales through orange-red to become light orange when fully grown (diameter to 20cm/8in). Edges slightly cracked, and showing the yellow gills. Sometimes traces of the volva remain on the expanded cap.

**Gills** crowded, free, extremely fragile; an unmistakable rich yellow (the main identification characteristic: no other European *Amanita* has yellow gills). Spore print: white to pale yellow.

**Stem** to 3cm/1½ in diameter and 15cm/6in high. Yellow, normally still with yellow ring. Stem base encased in the bag-like volva.

**Flesh** orange-yellow under the cap, becoming white towards the centre and in stem. Firm-textured. Pleasant smell; sweet mushroomy taste.

**Habitat** open deciduous woodland in warm climates, especially with oak and chestnut. Occasionally under pine, particularly in Mexico (though it is not confirmed that the New World fungus is identical with that from Europe).

**Season** in Italy and France, from early summer to the beginning of October.

## CLEANING AND COOKING

Some Italian cook books use *Amanita caesarea* in stews, but because of its delicacy and rarity, I recommend that you eat small ones raw. The large ones are excellent grilled, and served with freshly made pasta.

Don't peel the cap – just wipe the surface if necessary, and brush any foreign bodies out of the gills. Check the stem for maggots: the base in particular may be infested and can be cut away, but the upper part is usually clear.

*Amanita caesarea* keeps relatively well for up to a week in a refrigerator.

# ARMILLARIA MELLEA

Honey Fungus/Bootlace Fungus

Fr: armillaire couleur de miel   G: Hallimasch   I: chiodini
P: opienka miodowa   Sp: armilaria color de miel   Sw: honungsskivling

I first started to gather *Armillaria mellea* when I was only eight. A railwayman who worked for my father showed me how and where to collect *famigliola* – the local name for this mushroom which grows in tight little 'family' clusters. In the late autumn I used to walk through the fields near my home in Borgofranco not caring whether the sun was shining or the fields were shrouded in mist and fog, so great was my pleasure in the search. The local farmers had no objection to my tramping across their land because the mushrooms I was gathering grew at the base of young trees, and would otherwise have killed them. *Armillaria mellea* is a lethal parasite of most trees, but in particular of the willows that divided the local fields and whose supple young branches were perfect for tying up the newly pruned vines in spring. It was a great thrill for a young boy to walk from tree to tree gathering the mushrooms, and I would return home with full baskets, proud that I was contributing to the family larder. My mother always used them to make a wonderful meal for us.

In autumn you can always find the inexpensive 'famigliole' at local markets in Italy and France – side by side with the very expensive porcini, ovoli and tartufi.

White gills easily distinguish honey fungus from its look-alike, sulphur tuft (*Hypholoma fasciculare*), whose gills are dull sulphur-yellow to greenish.

RECOGNITION

The name 'honey fungus' describes the colour rather than the smell or taste. The mushrooms grow in small tight clusters, with the caps very close together. The fungus spreads vegetatively by means of black rhizomorphs resembling bootlaces, hence the alternative name.

**Cap** variable 3–20cm/1½–8in, hemispherical becoming flattened, with depressed centre. Pale honey-yellow to brown or ochre to dark brown, with stronger colour concentration at centre. Young specimens usually have a few rather fibrillose scales at the centre.

**Gills** white, becoming creamy with age; adnate to slightly decurrent. Spore print: creamy-white.

**Stem** tall and thin in relation to cap (1.5cm/¾in diameter but up to 20cm/8in tall). White in young specimens, later becoming similar in colour to cap. Becomes woody with age. Cottony 'ring' just below cap.

**Flesh** white, with mushroomy but not particularly pleasant smell. Taste is slightly bitter

and astringent. (After blanching both smell and taste improve dramatically.)

**Habitat** parasitic, growing in large clusters at the base of deciduous trees, including olive but mainly beech, willow, poplar, mulberry, etc, and on stumps and submerged roots.

**Season** mid summer to late autumn.

CLEANING AND COOKING

This is one of my favourite mushrooms to eat with spaghetti. It is delicious sautéed in butter and garlic, and excellent in stews and soups or cooked with other mushrooms. Good for preserving as a pickle and 'au naturel', but not recommended for freezing.

This mushroom is really rewarding for collectors, because it is fairly common and when you do find it, it is usually in large quantities. Do not eat it raw – it is mildly toxic, but once cooked it is perfectly safe. Blanch for at least 5 minutes at a high temperature, and discard the cooking water.

Discard the woody stems of older specimens.

# BOLETUS BADIUS

Bay Bolete

F: cèpe bai    G: Maronenröhrling    I: boleto baio
Sp: boleto bajo

This relative of the more popular *Boletus edulis* – by no means a 'poor relation' – is very rewarding, not only for the frequency with which it grows and the pleasure derived from looking for it, but also for its versatility in the kitchen. It is one of the most common edible wild mushrooms found in European countries with a moderate climate and so is the mushroom I proudly take with me (obviously, in its dried form) when I go back to Italy to visit my family. My mother always finds plenty of use for it in the kitchen, although the local 'porcini' have a more intense flavour. The eyes of my relations open wide with incredulity whenever I tell them how I find this mushroom in such huge quantities. I still find it pretty incredible myself: once after a successful 'hunt' my wife and I had to build piles of them at the side of the path and pick them up later; we filled the boot of the car with them, and still left plenty for other people to gather.

Not every year is such a productive one, of course, but you very often find some of these boletes growing in woodland – especially beneath pines, where the forest floor is relatively free from undergrowth. Sometimes they are difficult to find because of the camouflage of pine needles, cones and dead branches; sometimes ferns hide the mushrooms beneath their fronds, but where these are not too dense you can brush them aside with your stick. The clue to their whereabouts has been given to me many times by the caps the squirrels leave lying on the forest floor after they have consumed the stems. The ideal weather conditions are three to four days after some rain which has followed a warm spell.

On one occasion Paul Levy and Roger Phillips organized through the *Observer* a sort of studying and tasting foray in the woods of Blenheim Palace. I knew that a hunt of that kind would not produce enough specimens to satisfy dozens of people, so I paid a visit to one of my secret places the day before, and collected a big basketful of magnificent specimens of *Boletus badius*. After the foray we returned to Paul's house, where I sautéed the mushrooms in butter with garlic and parsley – to the delight of all the participants, including the very professional palate of Jane Grigson. This was my contribution to the delicious meal we prepared between us. It was a glorious October day, and I can still remember the friendly atmosphere in Paul's house and, above all, the taste of the wonderful apple pie produced by Jane.

## RECOGNITION

**Cap** nearly spherical at first, almost merging with stem. Very small specimens have a deep brown velvety sheen, which becomes slippery when wet. When fully grown, cap flattens and colour pales to ochraceous brown but retains its leathery feeling. When very old, cap tends to curve slightly, particularly at the rim, exposing more of the pores. Diameter usually 12–14cm/about 5–6in, occasionally larger.
**Pores** cream to pale yellow in young specimens, turning yellowish green with age. In older specimens the pores can be seen quite distinctly and turn blue-green when bruised. Spore print: yellowish brown.
**Stem** usually paler than cap, with vertical streaking; cylindrical, sometimes curved and tapering at base.
**Flesh** firm, creamy-white to pale yellow. In mature specimens, turns slightly blue when cut or touched. Delicate aroma.
**Habitat** on soil, in coniferous and deciduous woodland.
**Season** mid summer to late autumn.

## CLEANING AND COOKING

The blue discoloration of the flesh is one of the reasons many people avoid eating this

mushroom, believing it to be poisonous, but it is in fact quite delicious – especially if your specimens are young, with firm flesh and a fresh aroma. You have to inspect older specimens with some care as they can contain maggots, though in general the species is remarkably maggot-free. Avoid washing, as the pores soak up water: just wipe if dirty.

Boletus badius can be found on the market stalls of most European countries, and its uses are very similar to those for B. edulis. Small specimens are delicious raw, sliced very thinly for salads. They make a wonderful accompaniment to any sort of meat or fish, and are exceptionally good sautéed in butter with garlic and parsley. They can be frozen or pickled; dried ones have a very delicate and subtle flavour, and can be used in all sorts of soups and sauces.

# BOLETUS EDULIS
Cep/Penny Bun

A: Herrenpilz   F: cèpe   G: Steinpilz   I: porcino   P: borowik szlachetny
R: prawdziwek; byelii greeb   Sp: boleto comestible   Sw: Karljohan

*Boletus edulis* represents the wild mushroom par excellence. This is what most Europeans mean when they talk about 'wild mushrooms', and it was popular enough in the pre-inflationary days of Victorian Britain to be given the appropriate nickname of 'penny bun' because of its well-baked colour and round shape. The Romans called this mushroom 'suillus', Latin for 'pig' – a name echoed in the contemporary Italian 'porcino'; some say this is because pigs like them, some that the young specimens look like fat little piglets. In Germany the common name means 'stone mushroom' – descriptive like 'penny bun', but in Austria it is known as 'the gentleman's mushroom', while in Sweden it has the curious name of 'Karljohan'.

Some mycophiles may claim to prefer the rare *Amanita caesarea* or the morel, but the cep remains the safest to collect, the tastiest and the most rewarding in the kitchen of all wild mushrooms – quite simply, 'the best'. Since it is commercially collected and sold both fresh and dried it is one of the most sought-after wild mushrooms. Because of the delicacy of its flavour and its versatility, this is the mushroom that the world's leading chefs make most use of, creating many wonderful dishes.

## RECOGNITION

**Cap** at first hemispherical, becoming flatter when mature. Usually 8–20cm/3–8in diameter; occasionally to 30cm/12in. Cuticle smooth, colour varying from pale to dark brown.

**Pores** closely packed and off-white at first, turning pale to dark yellowish green in older specimens, with tubular pore structure clearly visible. Spore print: olive brown.

**Stem** in very young specimens stem and cap seem to merge together in almost spherical shape; later, stem grows to club-like shape, slightly broader at base, to 12.5cm/5in diameter. No ring. Sometimes the stem develops larger than the cap, and tends to become riddled with maggots. Colour below cap is pale brown, becoming almost white towards base, with surface covering of white reticulum or network.

**Flesh** in cap, off-white and firm; no discoloration when bruised. Stem flesh whiter, becoming woody and fibrous with age. Aroma: delicate and musty, though less intense in mushrooms found in temperate climates than in those growing in Mediterranean areas.

**Habitat** in grass in or near mixed woodland (pine, oak, beech, birch and chestnut); usually singly, sometimes in groups of two or three. One of the most likely places is along a golf course, especially where the fairways are bordered with heather which in turn gives on to woodland. I have found ceps on pure sand and on bare soil – but never far from the roots of at least one of the trees that are supposed to nurture them.

**Season** early summer to first frosts.

## CLEANING AND COOKING

The smaller specimens are suitable for pickling and freezing as well as cooking fresh, and may be thinly sliced and eaten raw in salads. Whole caps of mature ceps are good grilled, as in Italy. The older specimens are best sliced and fried or used in stews and sauces. Ceps are excellent dried, and give a very distinctive aroma to sauces and stews in which they are used; adding a small quantity to blander mushrooms enhances their flavour immensely and is an economical way of using expensive bought dried ceps.

When you collect this mushroom, take hold of the stem near the base and twist to left and right to ease it away from the mycelium. If you cut it free with a knife there is said to be a danger with such large-stemmed mushrooms that the part left in the ground will eventually rot and destroy the

mycelium, preventing further fruit-bodies from growing in that spot. Do use your knife, though, to clean the dirt from the stem base before you put the mushroom in your basket.

Don't peel ceps, and certainly don't wash them – just wipe off any dirt. Some people discard the pores if they have become soft. Cut larger mushrooms in half to check for maggots. If you intend drying the ceps, don't let a few maggots worry you: they will just disappear when the ceps are sliced and dried. Dry the bits and pieces as well as the good slices, to make into savoury powder.

# CANTHARELLUS CIBARIUS

## Chanterelle

A: Eierschwamm    F: chanterelle comestible; girolie    G: Pfifferlinge   I: gallinaccio; cantarello; finferlo
P: pieprznik jadalny   Sp: rebozuelo   Sw: kantarell

The delicate aroma of apricots and wonderful golden-yellow colour make the chanterelle a beautiful and graceful mushroom. Like *Boletus edulis* and *B. badius*, this is one of the most popular edible wild mushrooms, well known to leading chefs all over the world. The colour, texture and shape of *Cantharellus cibarius* are unique, and in America there is even a deep blue version: can you imagine what a wonderfully exotic sight a dish with both colours would make?

My wife Priscilla loves this mushroom. She seems to be a natural chanterelle detector when we are out on forays, and usually spots them long before I do, even in autumn when the task is made more difficult by the yellow and brown leaves that have fallen from the birch trees. She tells me of the enormous pleasure she takes in easing them from their mossy bed with her fingers.

It is a fairly common mushroom, especially in Scotland where I have heard that they sometimes literally cover the ground. I know of one young boy who increases his pocket money quite substantially in the season by collecting large quantities and sending them to France, where people are prepared to pay a great deal of money to enjoy them.

One day, my heart heavy with sorrow, I had to watch my best chanterelle ground disappearing between the ferocious teeth of an excavator preparing the way for a motorway. Every time I drive over that spot I remember how beautiful the mushrooms were, growing in luxurious moss. That's progress.

RECOGNITION

**Cap** in small specimens at first convex and minute, becoming funnel-shaped when mature, with thin and irregular rim. To 8cm/3in diameter. Deep yolk-yellow to pale yellow, fading with age.
**Gills** resembling irregular branching folds or veins, decurrent from top almost to base of stem. Not crowded, quite irregular. Concolorous with cap. Spore print: pale yellow.
**Stem** thick and wide, tapering towards base to form narrow lower part of funnel. To 2–3cm/ about 1in diameter at base, and 6cm/2½ in tall in large specimens.

**Flesh** pale yellow, firm, with peppery taste. Fresh smell, faintly of apricots. No discolouring on bruising, and usually maggot-free.
**Habitat** in mixed woods, often among moss, solitarily or in groups on soil.
**Season** summer to late autumn.

CLEANING AND COOKING

This mushroom is very versatile, and its colour is fabulous for decorative purposes. It is always good if eaten fresh, but keeps well in a refrigerator for a maximum of four to five days in a basket covered with a damp cloth. It can be eaten raw – its rather peppery taste disappears on cooking. It tastes at its best with scrambled eggs or in soups and stews, and is excellent for sauces. It is good for pickling, but does not freeze or dry so well.

Because it loses some of its flavour if washed, I suggest you clean it thoroughly with a brush when you collect it to prevent sand or grit from getting lodged in the gills.

# COPRINUS COMATUS

Shaggy Ink Cap/Lawyer's Wig/Shaggy Mane/Inky Cap

A & G: Schopftintling    F: coprin chevelu; goutte d'encre    I: agarico chiomato
P: czernidłak kołpakowaty    R: navoznik byelii    Sp: barbuda    Sw: fjalig blaksvamp

The shape of *Coprinus comatus* always makes me think of a white version of the bearskins that the guards at Buckingham Palace wear. You see these mushrooms in groups along roads and paths, in parks and pastures. Once at the sight of a glorious troop of them I stopped my car suddenly, much to the consternation of the motorists behind me. They were growing among luxuriously rich grass just outside the main gate of an army barracks – it was as if they were standing on guard at the gate. With a wave of apology to the other motorists, I proceeded to collect them – much to the astonishment of the onlooking human soldiers.

The various English names appropriately describe different characteristics. The scales on the cap indeed resemble the curls on a lawyer's wig, and the cap has a tendency to deliquesce into a black fluid which in past ages was used as a source of ink for writing.

These are very delicate-tasting members of the Agaric family and, in my opinion, resemble field mushrooms in flavour. They are perhaps underestimated by chefs: I have made some experiments in cooking these mushrooms, with excellent results, and find them versatile. Only the small specimens are of any value, while the gills are still white; once the cap and gills start to darken, they are of no use.

RECOGNITION

**Cap** acutely ovate or cylindric in young specimens, growing 3–15cm/1¼–6in tall and 1–6cm/⅜–2½in in diameter and closed towards the stem; the white cuticle is covered in large white scales with brownish tips, with a touch of light brown at the top. As the mushroom matures, the cap opens to a bell shape and the off-white cuticle becomes first grey then black from the rim upwards, as auto-digestion takes place and the cap turns to an inky black pulp.
**Gills** in young specimens visible only by cutting the cap lengthways. Very crowded and tightly packed. At first white, turning pink, then grey and finally black. Spore print: brownish black.
**Stem** long, thin and hollow, 1–3cm/⅜–1¼in in diameter and up to 25cm/12in tall. White. Membrane protecting young gills remains on the stem in the form of an irregular ring, or breaks loose and falls to the base.
**Flesh** when very young the stem and cap form a sturdy body with very firm delicate white flesh. Smell very fresh and mushroomy, not dissimilar to that of old field mushrooms. Much to the delight of the gatherer, insect larvae do not seem to infest this mushroom as the caps disappear too quickly.
**Habitat** occasionally isolated, but usually gregarious – sometimes in huge groups. Occurs almost anywhere – on hard soil along country lanes and bridleways; where soil has been disturbed; in lawns and pastures.
**Season** late summer to late autumn, especially in

warm but not *too* humid weather: this mushroom can go from button to deliquescence in two days, even less in warmer conditions.

CLEANING AND COOKING

Use only small firm specimens, with the cap still closed around the stem (mature specimens would be too mushy in texture, and the ink would colour black everything with which it came into contact). The caps quickly open out and mature once cut, so do not keep them too long. If you are not able to use them straight away, I suggest blanching them to keep them for a couple of days. You can wash closed caps to remove sand.

*Coprinus comatus* is simply delicious however you prepare it. Deep-fry the smaller 'buttons' after dipping them in beaten egg and rolling them in breadcrumbs. They are very good for stews, soups and sauces, and for sautéing in butter with chives and parsley. The lack of a distinct flavour/aroma means they are not really suitable for the freezing or drying processes.

# CRATERELLUS CORNUCOPIOIDES

### Horn of Plenty (UK)/Black Trumpet (USA)

A: Totentrompete   F: trompette des morts   G: Herbsttrompete   I: trombetta dei morti
P: lejkowiec dęty   Sp: trompeta de los muertos

Of all the European names for this mushroom, I like the British 'horn of plenty' best. This fragile mushroom does indeed look like a cornucopia – or, perhaps, a black trumpet. Most of the other descriptions sound too funereal to suit the mushroom; although it is indeed grey to black in colour, it has none of the connotations of death that so many of the names suggest.

It is in fact a very good and tasty mushroom that can be widely used in cooking. When I first introduced it on the menu in my restaurant, clients were somewhat reluctant to eat it because of its black colour. Now, however, it is becoming one of the favourites, and in season I produce some very elegant and delicious dishes by cooking it together with a delicate white fish such as halibut, sole or monkfish.

## RECOGNITION

**Cap** very similar to the bell end of a trumpet: deeply funnel-shaped, with irregularly lobed and wavy margins; initially pale brown, then grey and finally black. To 8–10cm/3–4in diameter.
**Gills** almost non-existent; the forming of spores takes place on the hymenium situated on the ridged outer sides of the tubular stem. When ripe, the pores colour the stem white to grey, giving a velvety sheen.
**Stem** an irregular tube 1–2cm/⅜–¾ in in diameter and up to 12cm/4¾ in tall, with very thin walls.
**Flesh** externally grey, turning black when wet; internally darker grey. This mushroom is not very fleshy because of its thin, cartilaginous and fragile walls. A distinctive pleasant smell and particularly delicate taste and texture – in fact, it is known in some parts of Italy as the 'poor man's truffle'.
**Habitat** gregarious in leaf litter, especially in frondose woods, but preferring the presence of beech. Don't forget to mark on your map where you first find them, because they usually grow in the same spot every year.
**Season** late summer to late autumn.

## CLEANING AND COOKING

The horn of plenty is ideal for preparing sophisticated dishes requiring its black colour and delicate taste. It is delicious just sautéed in butter with parsley and chives, excellent for sauces and also very good in soups and stews. It is not recommended for freezing unless first cooked in butter. Ideal for drying and reducing to

powder, which is then used to improve the flavour of sauces. It is not particularly good for pickling, nor does it keep very long in its fresh state as it tends to dry out and become rather leathery.

Pay maximum attention to cleaning these mushrooms – small insects find their way deep into the funnel; if they are not dislodged by shaking, it may be best to cut the mushrooms lengthwise to clean them. This is one instance of a mushroom where washing is possible if the specimens are particularly dirty.

# FISTULINA HEPATICA

Ox Tongue/Beefsteak Fungus

A: Ochsenzunge    F: fistuline hépatique
G: Leberpilz    I: lingua di bue

# LAETIPORUS SULPHUREUS

(syn POLYPORUS SULPHUREUS)

Sulphur Polypore/Chicken of the Woods

F: polypore soufre    I: poliporo sulphureo

Of the many bracket fungi or polypores (so called for the many pores on the underside of the cap, from which the spores are released), only a few are edible, and most have a destructive effect on the trees they parasitize. As well as being appreciated gastronomically, *Fistulina hepatica* produces a particularly fine coloration of the oak wood on which it usually grows and which it eventually destroys.

They are called bracket fungi because they look like a bracket or shelf attached to the tree from which they obtain their nutrition. Hunting mushrooms does not always mean keeping your nose and eyes to the ground: although these mushrooms are usually found at the base of the trunk, they can grow *anywhere* on the host tree, so I'm afraid you will have to look a bit higher from time to time. (This means that as you progress through the wood looking up and down and from side to side, you will look like one of those awful nodding dogs one sometimes sees in the rear windows of cars.)

My friend Gennaro found one of the best specimens of *Laetiporus sulphureus* I have ever seen some 5 metres or 15 feet from the ground on the trunk of a willow, and had to return home to fetch his ladder. This fungus was enormous and of the most succulent quality, and was eventually used in soups and stews. On another occasion he collected a wonderful specimen from an even more precarious situation, a huge willow bough overhanging a lake. He had to borrow a boat from a party of weedcutters in order to

collect it – a hair-raising experience, since the boat was small and Gennaro is large.

I have chosen to 'bracket' these two species together here because their general characteristics are so unlike those of other mushrooms discussed.

RECOGNITION

*Fistulina hepatica*

**Cap** can reach a diameter of 35cm/14in and a thickness of 6–7cm/2½–2¾in. It is broadly tongue-shaped and when young is very soft and juicy with minute warts covering the top of the cap, which is brick-red – the whole very similar in appearance to an ox tongue. Margin rounded at first, becoming thinner as it ages.

**Pores** pinkish, closely packed. Pores visible and separate (unlike most polypores, where they are fused together), bruising darker when touched. Spore print: yellowish pink.

**Stem** either sessile, or attached by a short, thick almost indiscernible stem.

**Flesh** when cuticle is peeled away, flesh appears wet and of a brilliant red that deepens with age. Cutting reveals pale pink veinous streaks similar to some steak (hence 'poor man's meat'); flesh is heavy for its size and extremely succulent. Aroma pleasant, strong and mushroomy; taste slightly sour when raw.

**Habitat** deciduous woodland: prefers oak, sometimes sweet chestnut; on living trees or stumps.

**Season** late summer to late autumn.

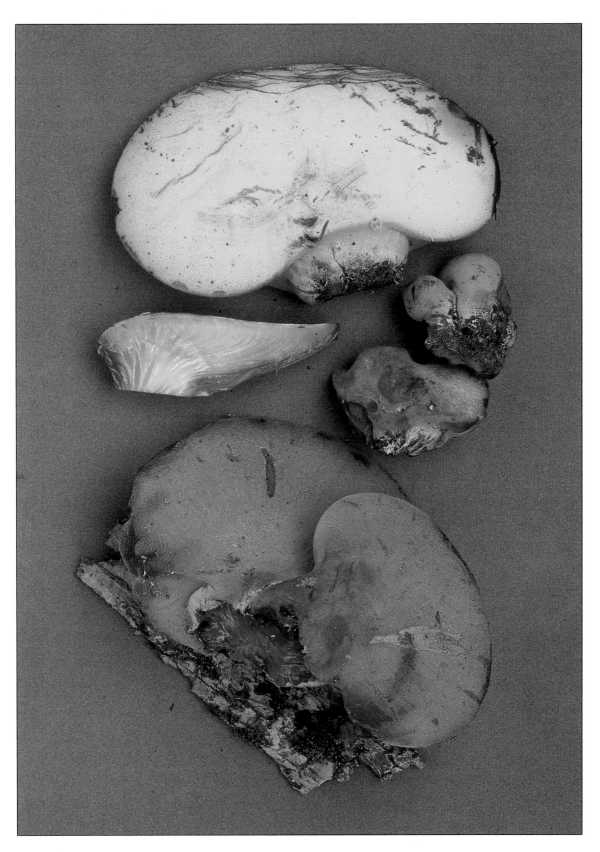

OX TONGUE OR BEEFSTEAK FUNGUS, *FISTULINA HEPATICA*

SULPHUR POLYPORE OR CHICKEN OF THE WOODS, *LAETIPORUS SULPHUREUS*

*Laetiporus sulphureus*

**Cap** brilliant sulphur-yellow, the cuticle very smooth and suede-like when young, becoming leathery later. Sessile, attached by growth to bark of host tree. Shape at first bud-like, later fan- or bracket-shaped; sometimes singly but often in tiered clusters that assume grotesque shapes and proportions. Fully mature specimens can reach 70cm/28in in diameter and weigh up to 22kg/ 50 lb (though they are too tough to be edible at this stage).

**Pores** visible only under magnification; concolourous with or slightly paler than cuticle, depending on age; bruising darker. Spore print: white.

**Flesh** extremely succulent, with fibrous structure similar to chicken meat. Young specimens exude moisture when squeezed (you sometimes see droplets of liquid – known as fungal guttation – exuding from surface, giving an aura of extreme freshness); flesh becoming white and crumbly with age. Aroma very mushroomy, sometimes even pungent; taste usually excellent, though sometimes sour.

**Habitat** deciduous woodland: prefers oak and willow; common on wild cherry and yew.

**Season** late spring to autumn. This mushroom continues to grow despite a lack of rain and appears fresh and succulent even in dry spells, presumably taking moisture from the host tree.

CLEANING AND COOKING

Both of these mushrooms can be slightly sour-tasting at times, so they should always be cooked to remove possible bitterness and ensure digestibility.

Each is similar to real meat in texture, being very fleshy and succulent, and so it can be prepared as such. Large slices from a tender specimen of *Laetiporus sulphureus* can be grilled or used as cutlets. When the specimen is more mature and the colour deepens to orange-yellow, it is excellent for soups, stews and pickling – but is not recommended for drying or for freezing (unless first cooked in butter).

*Fistulina hepatica*, which turns black when cooked, contains more acidity. Take this into account when cooking – it makes a good accompaniment to fatty or rich food such as sweetbreads or brains.

Since both mushrooms grow on trees they are usually fairly free from dirt and will just need brushing off. Cut away the base of *Laetiporus sulphureus* where it was attached to the tree, since splinters of bark are occasionally absorbed into the fruit-body.

A SUPERB SPECIMEN OF CHICKEN OF THE WOODS, *LAETIPORUS SULPHUREUS*

# HYDNUM REPANDUM

(syn DENTINUM REPANDUM)

## Hedgehog Fungus

F: pied de mouton    G: Semmelstoppelpilz    I: steccherino dorato
P: kolczak obtączasty    Sp: lengua de gato    Sw: blek taggsvamp

This excellent mushroom, commonly available in most European markets, has one distinctive characteristic: instead of the gills or pores that most of the other edible mushrooms have, the spore-producing hymenophore consists of spines pointing downwards from the underside of the cap – hence the name 'hedgehog'. As far as texture and taste are concerned, it is very similar in character to the chanterelle. It is quite common and relatively easy to find, even in seasons when other mushrooms may not be so plentiful. Because of its spines, this mushroom is one of the easiest to recognize. There are similar species with spines, but with darker colouring, making the 'hedgehog' quite safe to collect.

RECOGNITION

**Cap** irregular, very fleshy, brittle, convex to flat; from almost white through pale yellow to orange, depending on location. Up to 15cm/6in diameter. Cuticle very smooth, not viscid, but with a suede-like quality.

**Spines** very crowded, growing perpendicular to the underside of cap, decurrent, reaching maximum 6mm/¼ in. Extremely fragile, breaking at slightest touch. Usually concolorous with cap. Spore print: white.

**Stem** large, more pronounced towards the base, often eccentric to cap. Colour paler than rest of mushroom and surface as smooth as cap. To 7cm/2¾in high and 4cm/1⅝ in diameter.

**Flesh** fleshy and quite firm, but brittle; of a whitish yellow and slightly bitter in taste: when cooked, bitterness disappears and mushroom is tasty with pleasant aroma.

**Habitat** gregarious, sometimes in rings or strips, under trees in coniferous or broad-leaved woodland.

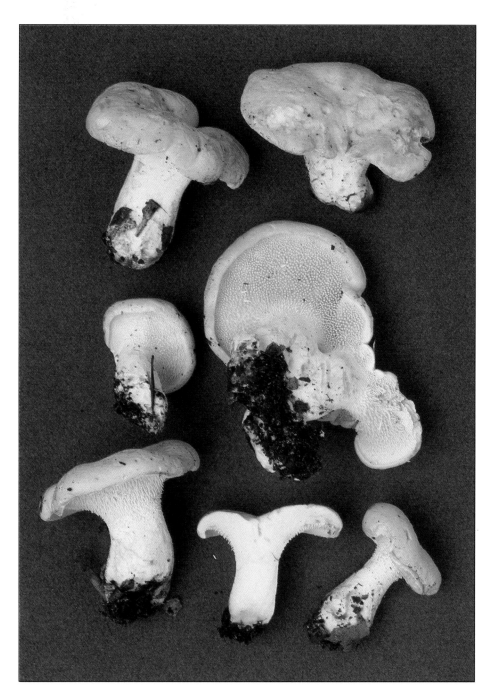

**Season** mid summer to late autumn in mild weather.

CLEANING AND COOKING

The younger specimens are very rewarding, as the whole mushroom can be used, including the spines; in older specimens these should be removed, as they can add to the bitterness. This mushroom should always be cooked, to remove any hint of bitterness in the flesh. It can be eaten by itself, stewed or fried in butter with onions, and also with other mushrooms. The flesh is of firmer consistency than that of the chanterelle, making it good for drying and using later in sauces and soups. It is also excellent pickled, and once cooked may be frozen. It is one of the mushrooms least likely to be infested with maggots, and is easily cleaned with a scrape of a knife or a light brushing. It can be kept in the refrigerator for a few days without deteriorating.

# LACTARIUS DELICIOSUS

Saffron Milk Cap (UK)/Delicious Milk Cap (USA)

A & G: Blutreizker    Fr: lactaire délicieux    I: agarico delizioso
P: mleczaj rydz    Sp: nizcalo de abetal    Sw: tallblodriska

As the names 'Lactarius' and 'milk cap' suggest, the members of this genus exude a milky substance when broken or cut; this liquid may remain white or may turn orange or wine-coloured, depending on the species. Two major features clearly distinguish L. deliciosus: the milky fluid exuded immediately becomes a deep reddish-orange, and the saffron-orange flesh slowly turns green when bruised.

There are many other edible species of Lactarius, especially in America, ranging from purple to indigo-blue in colour, but in Europe L. deliciosus is one of the few considered excellent and worth collecting. Many people, including French, Germans, Poles, Swedes and Russians, feel passionately about this mushroom. I love it for its nutty taste and firm texture, but above all for the brilliant colour which looks wonderful in special dishes. During the season a young Polish man who lives in Wales sends me a regular supply with which I create the exquisite dishes that delight my customers.

When collecting, take extra care to distinguish this mushroom from the poisonous Lactarius torminosus (woolly milk cap). The main superficial difference is the coarse woolly covering to the cap (and especially the cap margin) of L. torminosus; the colour of its flesh is white, and the milk exuded remains white. In addition, L. torminosus grows among birch woods, while L. deliciosus is restricted to conifers.

## RECOGNITION

**Cap** at first convex, with a small depression at the centre becoming larger and deeper as the margin, which is initially rolled, expands to form a large shallow funnel. Smooth cuticle first orange-saffron (often with concentric narrow zones alternating lighter and darker saffron, which fade with maturity); later paler and rather dull; tending to turn green when bruised. Diameter to 15cm/6in.

**Gills** same colour as cap, turning green when bruised. Very crowded, slightly decurrent, fragile. Spore print: pale yellowish.

**Stem** hollow, relatively short and thick (to 7cm/2¾in high and 4cm/1⅝in diameter). Colour paler than cap or gills, and flecked with orange spots, especially towards base; also discolouring green.

**Flesh** when cut or broken all parts exude a milky latex which rapidly turns carrot-orange in contact with air. Slightly bitter taste (disappears on cooking).

**Habitat** among short grass in coniferous woods, often nestling beneath pine needles (with stem hidden and only the characteristic 'zoned' cap visible). Occasionally solitary; usually gregarious.

**Season** late summer to late autumn.

## CLEANING AND COOKING

This mushroom has an 'al dente' texture and a not-too-distinctive flavour; to my palate it is delicious, given some attention in its preparation. First of all, check for maggots: older specimens may be infested, so cut these lengthways down the stem for closer inspection and cleaning. These mushrooms are firm enough to rinse in water if they are particularly dirty or gritty. Next, blanch for 2–3 minutes to remove any bitterness. After this operation, use raw in salads; steam, stew or fry; or use in sauces for pastas, meat and fish. It freezes well. The Russians preserve this mushroom in salt (see page 119).

# Langermannia Gigantea

(syn LYCOPERDON GIGANTEUM; CALVATIA GIGANTEA)

### Giant Puffball

F: vesse de loup géante    G: Riesenboviste    I: vescia maggiore

I was once walking in Hyde Park with my dog Jan on an autumn day when I glimpsed a white football partly hidden among some shrubs near the path. I looked around expecting to see some children looking for it, but no one was. My attention was then drawn to a smaller ball next to the big one, which immediately gave me the clue that maybe this was a giant puffball – and, of course, this is what it turned out to be: a superb example of *Langermannia gigantea*, whose habitat, according to the books, is open fields.

This is where we found it in profusion on our way home from photographing the location shots for the cover of this book. I had to stop the car abruptly after spotting a field literally covered with giant puffballs, and photographer Andrew Whittuck, who was seeing them for the first time, could not believe his eyes at their size and sheer numbers. Now we had the problem of how to collect them: all our baskets were already full of mushrooms. Incredibly, there in the ditch alongside the road was a metal supermarket basket just waiting to be filled. Left there by Lady Luck, no doubt.

Of the many species of edible puffballs, the giant one is obviously the most rewarding as well as the most distinctive; one prime specimen is enough to provide a good meal for the whole family. The other species such as *Lycoperdon perlatum* and *L. pyriforme* need to be collected in far greater amounts, since each specimen seldom amounts to more than a mouthful. All the puffballs are good to eat while the flesh is firm and white, but the smaller ones need to be distinguished from the common earth-ball, *Scleroderma citrinum*, which is inedible, and *A. phalloides* in the unopened-egg stage.

RECOGNITION

*Langermannia gigantea* has neither cap, gills nor stem; it is a gasteromycete, with a subglobular fruiting body measuring up to 80cm/30in in diameter, its spores developing internally and 'puffing' out of the top when mature. It is attached to its mycelium by a sort of fragile root which eventually breaks, leaving the puffball free to be blown about the fields by the wind, disseminating its millions of spores. It looks like a ping-pong ball at first, grows to the size of a tennis ball, and finally attains the size of a football, at least – a truly sporting life.

The outer skin or exoperidium is quite firm and slightly leathery in texture, initially white and turning brown with age.

The flesh or gleba is also white and firm at first, then yellow and finally completely brown and powdery. Spores: dark yellowish brown. The smell of the fresh flesh is wonderfully mushroomy, like a field mushroom but slightly stronger-tasting.

**Habitat** on well-manured fields, in gardens and parks; on grass or among shrubs and nettles.
**Season** late summer to late autumn.

CLEANING AND COOKING

In Italy this very good and tasty mushroom is prepared in the same way as veal cutlets and, funnily enough, the flavour is quite similar. The firm flesh is wonderful sliced and deep-fried or grilled, as well as in soups. It is not good for drying, but can be sliced or cubed and pickled. Do remember, only the young specimens with firm white flesh can be eaten.

The surface may need wiping to remove grass and earth; otherwise all the cleaning that needs to be done is to trim away the point at the base where the puffball was attached to its 'root'.

# LECCINUM VERSIPELLE

(syn BOLETUS VERSIPELLIS; B. TESTACEOSCABER; LECCINUM TESTACEOSCABRUM)

### Orange Birch Bolete

F: bolet orangé   G: Rotuappe; Birkenpilz   I: porcinello rosso
P:koźlarz pomarańczowo żółty   Sw: tegelrod björksopp

If any mushroom can be considered to have a 'phallic' image, the young specimens of *Leccinum versipelle* possess this quality par excellence, sometimes even assuming grotesque proportions! You usually spot the orange cap of this bolete from quite a distance, and on parting the grass to pick it, you may be surprised by the length of the solid stem. In a good season my basket can be full in minutes, and the problem then is to carry them back to the car, since they are very heavy indeed.

If you discover a secluded place that people rarely visit, you may find mature specimens with caps as large as 30cm/12in in diameter, but these are usually so soft and spongy (and so infested with insect larvae) that the only useful thing to do is to break them up into pieces and scatter them around in the hope of assisting in disseminating the spores. I have a fabulous place for this mushroom, which likes to grow beneath birch trees, among tall luxurious grass and darker green heather with beautiful pink flowers. I hope that you too will be able to discover such a source. Unfortunately I must keep 'my' location secret because it is on common land, open to all but visited by few. It is situated in a depression and tends to retain any rainwater that may fall; in warmer weather, when the surrounding area has dried out, 'my' place is still moist and humid, providing this mushroom with the perfect environment.

Incidentally, when you do discover one of these mushrooms take care while picking it: sometimes younger specimens will be found growing close to the base of the stem. Search the surrounding area carefully, too, because if there is one, there are usually more to be found.

Poles and Russians in particular love this mushroom and cook it in many ways; some of them even prefer it to *Boletus edulis*.

RECOGNITION

**Cap** hemispherical at first, growing to maximum 30cm/12in diameter and becoming largely convex. At first very solid and a rich reddish orange, becoming quite soft and paler orange on maturing.
**Pores** minute in young specimens; grey-white, becoming darker grey to ochraceous later but also very spongy. Spore print: yellow-brown.
**Stem** almost as distinctive as cap: off-white with brown or black scabrous scales. To maximum 5cm/2in diameter and 25cm/10in tall, tapering towards cap.
**Flesh** both cap and stem in young specimens are very firm, almost hard, but tender. When mature the flesh of the cap becomes white and slightly spongy, and the stem becomes more fibrous, both turning greyish blue when cut. The smell is freshly mushroomy and the taste pleasant.
**Habitat** usually solitary, sometimes in groups, among rich ground vegetation beneath scrub birch.
**Season** early summer in humid weather to end of autumn.

There are several species of *Leccinum*. After *L. versipelle* the most delectable is *L. aurantiacum* (aspen bolete), which is similar in structure and cap colour but has reddish (rather than black) scales on the stem and is associated with Aspen. *L. quercinum* differs only in having a slightly darker cap than *L. aurantiacum* and in occurring with oak. The common birch bolete, *L. scabrum* is the least valuable: its cap is brown in colour, it is much slighter in structure, and can be slightly watery, with only a mild mushroom flavour and aroma. I should add, however, that both *Leccinum aurantiacum* and *L. quercinum* are comparatively rare (*L.aurantiacum* is very rare in Britain) and will never be found in the same quantities as *L. versipelle*.

CLEANING AND COOKING

As *Leccinum versipelle* is fairly moist and lacks a particularly intense aroma, I would not suggest

drying. It is, however, good for freezing from the raw state, and it pickles well, though the colour turns dark grey. Above all, I recommend it sliced and fried or sautéed in butter and garlic, or stewed; it is also extremely good for soups and sauces. It is a good 'bulking' mushroom, useful for quantity rather than quality.

I suggest peeling the cuticle off the cap, and always peel the stem with a sharp knife and discard the scales. Check for any insect larvae present, and discard any older specimens whose pores have become watery. Finally, do not worry if this mushroom turns almost black after cooking – it will still be delicious.

# LEPIOTA PROCERA

## PARASOL MUSHROOM

F: lepiote élevée; coulmelle    G: Parasolpilz    I: mazza da tamburo
P: czubajka kania    Sp: apagador    Sw: stolt fjällskivling

While the Italian name for this mushroom means 'drumstick', after the similarity between the young specimens and the drumsticks that drummers in brass bands use, all the other countries name it 'parasol', after the mature specimens, which look just like huge sunshades or parasols. Considering the differences in the weather, and the British love of brass bands, I would have thought the Italian and British names would be more apt if reversed.

The parasol mushroom is an Agaric with a distinctive appearance, and is quite easy to find and to recognize. It is one of the best and tastiest of the edible mushrooms, and is quite safe to collect if you follow the exact description. You need to distinguish it from its relative *Lepiota rhacodes* or the shaggy parasol, which has more woolly scales on top of the cap, a shorter stem and red-staining flesh. This species is believed to have caused some gastric upsets in sensitive stomachs, so it is best to keep to the simple parasol, *L. procera*.

## RECOGNITION

**Cap** at first ovate, with a veil sealing the rim to the stem. When the cap opens the veil breaks away and remains loosely on the stem as a whitish-brown ring. Fully grown cap has concentric brownish scales around the centre, where there is a definite nipple or umbo, and underlying colour is whitish. To 25cm/10in diameter.

**Gills** free and crowded, white, very broad (accounting for two-thirds of the cap's thickness); resembling pages of an open book. Spore print: white.

**Stem** to 30cm/12in tall and 2cm/¾ in diameter (4cm/1½ in at bulbous base); ridiculously thin, apparently not strong enough to support the cap; but tough, because woody and fibrous, and hence inedible. Initially greyish, becoming white later with brownish scales or snake-like markings. Veil remains loosely on hollow stem as large double ring.

**Flesh** thin flesh of cap is white, at first firm, becoming soft with age. No colour change on cutting or bruising. Pleasant smell and taste.

**Habitat** solitarily on soil, sometimes in small groups; in drier parts or margins of deciduous woods (with no particular tree preference); also open fields, gardens, hedgerows.

**Season** periodically from mid summer to autumn.

## CLEANING AND COOKING

The stem is too tough to be edible, but depending on the stage of growth, the cap can be cooked in many different and delicious ways. When it is small and still closed (at the 'drumstick' stage), it can be dipped in batter and fried; it looks something like a small scotch egg, and is delicious. When it has opened into a sort of cup, it is ideal for stuffing prior to stewing. When it is

completely flat like an opened parasol, it can be coated in beaten egg and breadcrumbs and then fried, making a tasty meal in itself.

Parasol mushrooms are not particularly good for pickling or preserving, so I suggest that you eat any you find fresh.

This mushroom is usually free from any insect larvae – unless the specimen is too old for picking anyway. When cleaning, just brush away any residual earth or sand from the cap; avoid washing, since they readily absorb water and this dilutes the flavour.

# LEPISTA NUDA

(syn TRICHOLOMA NUDUM)

## Wood Blewit

F: pied-bleu  G: Violetter Ritterling  I: agarico nudo
P: gąsówka naga  Sp: tricoloma violeta

Mushrooms do not contain any of the chlorophyll that gives plants their green colouring, but they do have a wonderful assortment of other colours instead. *Lepista nuda* or wood blewit is one of the commonest and most exquisite edible wild mushrooms in Britain, and its colours range from bluish-lilac and violet to pale brown and buff. It is a very satisfying mushroom because it grows abundantly, is quite easy to recognize and is excellent to eat. *After* cooking, however – avoid the temptation to enjoy the beautiful colour raw in salads, because *Lepista nuda* does contain some toxic substance that can cause gastric upsets if eaten in large quantities. This mild toxicity is removed during the cooking process, after which the mushroom is perfectly safe and absolutely delicious.

These mushrooms often grow in large groups over a wide area, so that you can gather a substantial amount very quickly – though fallen leaves in the deciduous woods make them more difficult to find. Their season is later than that of many other mushrooms, continuing well into the winter.

## RECOGNITION

### Lepista nuda

**Cap** at first convex, expanding irregularly until the margin curls up exposing the gills. To maximum 12cm/5in diameter. First lilac-coloured, then brownish. The cuticle is very smooth, giving a moist impression even in dry weather.

**Gills** free or slightly sinuate, crowded, darker than the cap, soon fading and becoming buff. Spore print: pinkish.

**Stem** surface at first lilac-speckled or fibrillose, becoming pale with age. When cut, darker at the edges and paling towards the centre. To 3cm/ 1¼in diameter (tapering slightly towards top) and 10cm/4in tall.

**Flesh** in young specimens thick and firm; violet, becoming more greyish with age. When cut the flesh in older specimens has the appearance of being impregnated with water. Pleasant, fruity almost perfumed aroma; extremely tasty.

**Habitat** in small or large groups, sometimes covering wide area, in deciduous woodland, hedgerows, sometimes gardens.

**Season** relatively late, sometimes starting at the end of September and continuing into December or even into the New Year, despite frosts.

### Lepista Saeva

Its relative, the field blewit, can – as the name suggests – be found in fields, meadows and well-manured pastureland. It differs in having a very pallid cap; only the stem is a brilliant violet, hence its other common name of 'blue leg'. The taste is very similar.

## CLEANING AND COOKING

*Lepista nuda* is an excellent mushroom – the very thick moist flesh means that a satisfying meal can be made from just a few specimens. It is

wonderful by itself, simply cooked by the time-honoured method of stir-frying in butter with a little garlic and parsley. You can use it in stews or sauté it with other mushrooms, and it is particularly good in sauces accompanying meat or fish. It freezes well after initial cooking; it is very good for pickling and for preserving in oil. I dry it in my purpose-built mushroom-drying machine. In fact, this mushroom is one of the few that applies itself perfectly to any culinary process – but do remember that it *does* need cooking.

The blewits are usually fairly insect-free and clean – wipe the caps if necessary. Discard the tougher stems of older specimens. Since blewits tolerate cold weather, they keep well in the refrigerator for a few days.

# MORCHELLA ELATA & MORCHELLA ESCULENTA

Morels

F: morille; éponge    G: Speisemorchel    I: spugnola bruna; spugnola gialla
P: smardz stóżkowaty    Sp: colmenilla    Sw: toppmurklor

This much sought-after mushroom commands a very high price on the world's markets, and is not always readily available. Like the truffle, it belongs to the category of fungus known as the ascomycetes, and instead of having gills or pores, the spore-bearing hymenium lines the inside of the pits or honeycomb-like depressions of the cap. It is one of the first mushrooms to appear in early spring, sometimes by late March if it is mild. Italy, France, Switzerland, the American Mid-west (climates with a well-regulated seasonal cycle of cold – mild – hot – mild) are those that suit morels. The state of Minnesota even has its own Festival of the Morel to welcome the arrival of this valuable member of the fungus world.

Armed with the knowledge that morels will grow on burnt ground, some ultra-passionate morel 'hunters' from Provence deliberately set fire to woodland in the hope that the following spring they would see the cherished fruiting bodies popping out of the scorched earth.

I remember finding some morels among great stands of cane as a small boy at Castelnuovo Belbo (actually, I was never *that* small). I imagined I was in some great fairyland jungle. I soon came down to earth when I got home, where my mother and brothers subjected my collection to a thorough scrutiny to make sure that what I had gathered was the true morel. Experienced eyes can easily distinguish it from the poisonous *Gyromitra esculenta* (false morel), which also grows in spring, by the shape of the cap, which is fairly symmetrical in the edible morel, and distinctly lobed and contorted in the false one.

*Morchella esculenta* and *M. elata* are the two very best species of morel. They differ slightly in their shape, colour and size, but their general characteristics are the same.

## RECOGNITION

If you cut a morel in vertical section, you will see that the cap and stem grow together forming a single body.

**Cap** made up from many cup-like depressions or pits, giving the appearance of a rather irregularly open-pored sponge. Lining these depressions are the asci – microscopic sacs in which the spores are produced. In *M. elata* the cap is conical, dark brown in colour, becoming darker with age; the pits have a fairly regular lengthwise orientation; the cap reaches up to 5cm/2in in diameter and up to 10cm/4in tall. *M. esculenta* is more rounded, with the pits irregularly arranged, and is of a creamy-yellow colour at first, becoming pale brown or buff with age. It is usually larger than *M. elata*, reaching up to 15cm/6in tall. (As with all mushrooms, the measurements vary according to location: in America, naturally, they grow bigger!)

**Stem** pale off-white; cylindrical and hollow in both species, slightly more swollen towards the base. In *M. elata* reaches 3cm/1¼in diameter and up to 5cm/2in tall; in *M. esculenta* reaches 5cm/2in diameter and up to 9cm/3⅝in tall.

**Flesh** both cap and stem look and feel cartilaginous and fragile, but the flesh is crisp and moist to the touch. Flesh of *M. elata* is pale brown in the cap and white in the stem. That of *M. esculenta* looks more spongy, but is also crisp and firm; flesh colour is paler than that of the surface, and the stem is off-white. I believe the culinary attraction of this mushroom has to be attributed more to the appearance, texture and preparation than to its intrinsic taste and smell – which are just pleasantly and delicately perceptible.

**Habitat** prefers sandy soil with underlying chalk; given this criterion, it can be found in open shrubby woodland, on wood edges and banks, in pastures, orchards, wasteland – and on burnt ground.

**Season** late March to May, depending on weather.

## CLEANING AND COOKING

I have already used many superlatives to describe this mushroom, which can be served with any type of food. I would stress, though, that it should always be cooked – when eaten raw it proves indigestible to some people.

A SPECIES OF MOREL, *MORCHELLA ESCULENTA*

Morels are not usually infested with any insect larvae, but I would check the hollow inside, which may harbour some insects. Try to keep them clean when you collect them by cutting away the base, which tends to be full of sand, so that this does not find its way into the wrinkles of the caps when the specimen is placed in your basket. If sand does get into these folds (and some will probably be there anyway) then a longer and more thorough cleaning job is in store for you. Use a brush: washing is not really recommended, but may be used as a last resort.

This is one of the few mushrooms that regenerate very well from the dried state, and dried ones can be used in exactly the same way as fresh ones. I find they taste strangely of bacon. Although they are expensive, dried morels are becoming more readily available in stores if you are not lucky enough to pick and dry your own. They need 20 minutes' soaking in lukewarm water; you may have to cut off the stem base – and remember to filter any sand out of the soaking water. Morels also preserve well 'au naturel' and by pickling, but are not recommended for freezing. Obviously, however the best way to use them is fresh.

# PLEUROTUS OSTREATUS

Oyster Mushroom

F: pleurote en huitre   G: Austernseitling   I: fungo ostrica
P: boczniak ostrygowaty   SW: ostronmissling

Named after the oyster because of its shape and its greyish-blue colour, *Pleurotus ostreatus* is one of the few mushrooms that have been found suitable for cultivation. The domestic version of the oyster mushroom can be found in supermarkets, although I prefer the wild version, which has a stronger taste.

Its relative *P. cornucopiae* takes its name from its resemblance to a horn of plenty. Although the two mushrooms are different in shape and colour, I have purposely put them together here because of their very similar general characteristics and culinary uses. Breaking through the bark of fallen trees and stumps, these typical parasite fungi grow down into the structure, absorbing the life-giving substance, until the wood is reduced to worthless matter. Be careful with identification, however: there are mushrooms growing on stumps which are inedible or poisonous.

I have to thank Gennaro Contaldo for my initial introduction to *Pleurotus cornucopiae*. I first met Gennaro at the beginning of May, when he appeared in my restaurant carrying, to my astonishment, a basket full of these mushrooms, freshly picked. It is very rare to find them growing in England at this time of year, and to my amazement he presented them to me as a gift. He now brings me basket after basket, and since then we have become firm mycological friends.

## RECOGNITION

### *Pleurotus ostreatus*

**Cap** flat and round; lateral, resembling a shell or tongue. Upper surface varies in colour from blue-grey when small to pale brown when fully grown; also from pale cream to noisette. Skin quite shiny. To 16cm/6½in diameter.

**Gills** pale cream, not very crowded, decurrent. Spore print: lilac.

**Stem** excentric to lateral, or almost absent.

**Flesh** white and very tender in small specimens, becoming tougher. Taste/aroma indistinct.

**Habitat** parasitic on fallen and decaying trees, mostly beech, in parks and countryside. Often hidden by grass or nettles, so remember to carry a stick.

**Season** early summer in warm conditions to first frost (I have even found some in December).

### *Pleurotus cornucopiae*

This is distinctly funnel-shaped, and grows more upright than lateral. It has a more pronounced stem than in *P. ostreatus*, reaching 20cm/8in when several fruiting bodies are grouped together forming a cluster. The cap is round and concave to the centre, forming the shape of the cornucopia. The colour of the top varies from white to pale brown, depending on location. The flesh is white and the spore print pale lilac. Habitat as for *P. ostreatus* with a preference for oak and elm.

## CLEANING AND COOKING

These are not superior mushrooms in the culinary sense – they do not have an outstanding flavour – but they are versatile when cooked

*PLEUROTUS CORNUCOPIAE*

OYSTER MUSHROOM, *PLEUROTUS OSTREATUS*

fresh, and their availability in cultivation makes them useful for adding that extra mushroomy something to a dish. Sauté them with garlic and butter, deep-fry them dipped in egg and breadcrumbs, or use them in soups. They are worth preserving only if you pickle them in vinegar before bottling them in olive oil (see page 123); unless very small, they become too tough when frozen, and they lack the flavour to make them dry well.

A cleaning tip: inspect the larger ones carefully. Sometimes you will find maggots in the stems: if so, simply cut them off and enjoy the caps.

When buying cultivated oyster mushrooms, choose the smaller specimens – they are less watery.

# SPARASSIS CRISPA

## Cauliflower Fungus

F: clavaire crêpue   G: Krauseglucke   I: arricciata
P: szmaciak gałęzisty   Sp: clavaria rizada

Whenever I am walking through pinewoods during the autumn, I keep an eye on the base of the trunks, which is where this peculiar mushroom usually chooses to grow. If you find a large specimen (and they can grow very large) it will be enough to make a complete meal. It really does look like a cauliflower, and is quite as interesting in its culinary uses. Keep a keen look out for this mushroom, since you are very unlikely to find it for sale in shops and markets – it is only of value to the connoisseur!

## RECOGNITION

There is no cap in the normal sense of the word; the mushroom is built up of many cartilaginous flat lobes reminiscent of a 'brain coral', with a short, strong stem. (An alternative name is 'brain fungus'.) The fruit-body can grow in quite a short time and can envelop in its flesh anything that is lying within the area of its growth – many times when cutting one open I have found pine needles and even small pine cones incorporated in the flesh.

**Fruit-body** usually subglobular, very variable in size: 20–50cm/8–20in diameter. Flat irregular lobes coloured cream to pale noisette, darkening with age. Spores: white or pale yellow. Flesh fragile, more consistent towards centre. Smell pleasant; taste sweet, nutty.

**Habitat** coniferous woods, at tree bases and on stumps.

**Season** late summer to late autumn.

## CLEANING AND COOKING

Pick only specimens that are creamy-white (cauliflower-colour); any that have turned yellowish will be tough and indigestible. Cut into sections to check for dirt, insects and foreign bodies: a good wash before cooking is – for once – recommended.

*Sparassis crispa* is very versatile indeed to cook with. I have fried it, preserved it in oil, dried it and frozen it (and it is one of the handful of mushrooms that reconstitutes really well from dried), all with excellent results. It is very good for soups, either fresh or dried, and can be used in all sorts of stews and, of course, on its own. Used together with other mushrooms, it adds a certain sophistication to a dish through its appearance, texture and flavour.

# SUILLUS GREVILLEI

(syn BOLETUS ELEGANS)

Larch Bolete/Tamarack Jack

F: bolet élégant   G: Goldröhrling   I: boleto elegante; laricino
P: maślak zólty   Sp: boleto amarillo   Sw: lärksopp

# SUILLUS LUTEUS

(syn BOLETUS LUTEUS)

Slippery Jack

F: bolet couleur de terre   G: Butterpilz   I: boleto giallo
P: maślak zwyczajny Sp: boleto anillado smörsopp

LARCH BOLETE OR TAMARAK JACK, *SUILLUS GREVILLEI*

The characteristics and culinary properties of these two mushrooms are so similar that I am discussing them together here, although they are distinct in appearance. Both grow under conifers of different types, and both have a slippery cuticle (hence the name Slippery Jack), so mind where you put your feet! Neither exactly reaches the high point of culinary distinction, but both are plentiful and rewarding used in soups and stews together with other mushrooms.

The powers that be have decided to classify boletes such as these with glutinous caps in the genus *Suillus* – though they are still listed under *Boletus* in many books.

RECOGNITION

**Cap** hemispherical when young, closed underneath by a veil, later flattening to maximum 10–12cm/4–5in in diameter. As the mushroom develops the veil detaches itself from the cap and remains on the stem in the form of a ring or skirt. The cuticle is viscid with gluten when moist, shiny when dry. *Suillus grevillei* is yellow-orange when young, paler yellow later; *S. luteus* is chocolate-brown when young, brown to violaceous later.

**Pores** spongy and very absorbent. Lemon-yellow and slightly decurrent in *Suillus grevillei*; paler yellow and adnexed in *S. luteus*.

**Stem** golden-yellow above the pale yellow ring in *Suillus grevillei*, becoming darker yellow below with a brownish patterning. To maximum 3cm/1¼ in in diameter and 10cm/4in tall. In *S. luteus* the stem is concolorous with pores above the ring (which is whitish and pale purple beneath) and yellow-brown to brown below it.

**Flesh** soft and tender in both cases, lemon to

SLIPPERY JACK, *SUILLUS LUTEUS*

chrome in *Suillus grevillei* and pale yellow to white in *S. luteus*. No distinctive aroma.
**Habitat** *Suillus grevillei* grows exclusively under larch; *S. luteus* usually with Scots pines, particularly near footpaths and banks.
**Season** summer to late autumn.

CLEANING AND COOKING

The caps of these mushrooms are so viscid that any grit, leaves, pine needles and so on that comes into contact with them will adhere in the basket, so I recommend your removing the cuticle and ring as soon as you pick them. Both are generally relatively maggot-free.

Their lack of distinctive flavour and moist flesh puts them in the 'useful' rather than the 'sought-after' category. They are not good for preserving, since they freeze well only when cooked, are too moist and slight in flavour for drying, and the spongy flesh is not firm enough for pickling. Enjoy them in season when they are plentiful: they are at their best fresh, cooked alone in soups and stews or adding bulk to a mixture of other mushrooms.

# TUBER MAGNATUM

White Truffle

F: truffe d'Alba
G: weisse Truffel
I: tartufo d'Alba

# TUBER MELANOSPORUM

Perigord Truffle

F: truffe du Périgord
G: schwarze Truffel
I: tartufo nero

# TUBER AESTIVUM

Summer Truffle

F: truffe d'été
I: scorzone

SUMMER TRUFFLE, *TUBER AESTIVUM*

The only time a professional truffle hunter will take someone with him is when he is absolutely certain that his location will remain a secret. As I was only seven or eight years old and incapable of divulging the route to anyone, my father's friend Giovanin offered to take me with him on a truffle hunt. Giovanin appeared on the day wearing big gum boots and a real hunting jacket with a large game pocket on the back. He had with him a stick, a funny-shaped digging tool and a small mongrel called Fido.

I clearly remember my impression of the November woods, with the leafless branches reaching out into the fog as if to pull themselves out of the gloom. Something about the mysterious atmosphere fascinated me, and I have been a fanatical mushroom hunter ever since. Suddenly Fido became wildly excited and started running up and down, his nose to the ground, sucking in the scent of the truffles like an animated vacuum cleaner. When he stopped abruptly and began clawing at the ground, Giovanin had the sign he'd been waiting for: Fido had found a truffle. Giovanin gently pushed the dog aside, dug a small hole with his special tool and lifted out a wonderful specimen of *Tuber magnatum*. He brushed the earth from the truffle and put it gently in his game pocket. Only at this point did Fido receive his meagre reward of a small biscuit.

On another occasion, Giovanin gave me a truffle to take home. I was ecstatic. I was hooked, and I still am. I call truffles 'food of gods, kings and pigs'. Some truffles contain a chemical resembling the male pig's sex hormone, and the riper the truffle the stronger and more attractive (for the female pig) the scent. The Romans used pigs to locate truffles, but it was hard to prevent them from eating the object of their desire; the trained dogs used nowadays instead are easier to handle and can be dissuaded from eating the truffles they find.

Something of the same mystery still attaches to truffles. Although France and Italy have increased supplies for commerce by developing techniques of treating the roots of young oaks with truffle spores, it is still left to nature to produce what is and always has been the mushroom most sought after by gourmets. I was once asked to appear on a television programme dealing with the latest scientific innovations and use my expertise to assess the merits of a synthetic black truffle from Switzerland. After examining and tasting the product I had to state that if this was man's attempt to emulate nature then he had failed dismally: the soft liquorice-like substance was devoid of any taste or smell, and could at best be used for decoration on pâtés.

Brillat-Savarin called the Perigord truffle the 'black diamond', which could 'make women more tender and men more agreeable'. Aphrodisiac qualities have been attributed to the truffle throughout history. I personally think that the difficulties involved in finding something so rare and exquisite trigger off a demand which inflates the price to an unaffordable level, and this very process becomes a stimulation – almost a sensual experience. The fact that this delicacy sometimes reaches palates that cannot appreciate it is an old human story, applying not only to truffles but to most exotic food.

Of the many different varieties of truffles in the world, three are the most esteemed and precious: *Tuber magnatum* (the white Alba truffle); *T. melanosporum* (the black Perigord truffle) and *T. aestivum* (the summer truffle). The aroma of the first of these is very pungent indeed. I once had a phone call from the Customs and Excise Officers at Heathrow Airport warning me that a parcel of perishable food that had arrived for me from Turin was suspected of containing 'something that had gone off'. It was beyond the imagination of the poor officials that white truffles could possess such a penetrating aroma. When I collected the package even the police dogs were looking slightly disturbed by the smell.

Knowing of my obsession, a colleague of my wife's once promised to bring me back some truffles from Saudi Arabia, where apparently they grow in profusion in the desert. When they arrived my heart stopped at the sight of a big plastic bag full of large white truffles. On closer examination, however, my heart stopped again – this time with disappointment. There was no smell, no taste! I went from elation to despair in an instant. All that glisters is not gold.

## RECOGNITION

Truffles are ascomycetes with roundish fruit-bodies which develop underground in mycorrhizal association with certain trees. The folded hymenium appears as a marbling of fine veins in the flesh, and the spore-producing asci are situated in the darker part of the flesh. The intense aroma of the ripe spores attracts animals to the fruit-body, which they grub up and eat, dispersing the spores by means of their droppings.

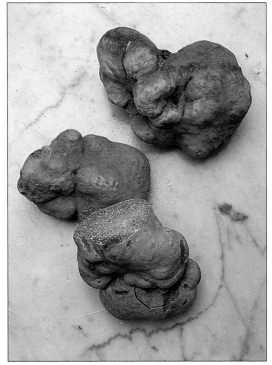

WHITE TRUFFLE, *TUBER MAGNATUM*

### Tuber magnatum

Grows in symbiosis with oak, hazel, poplar, beech, exclusively in Langhe area of Piedmont, of which the town of Alba is the centre (hence 'Alba truffle'). Irregular potato-like tuber has smooth skin from creamy yellow to pale hazel; the flesh is from pale cream to pale brown, marbled with white veins; occasionally with bright red spots, especially when growing with hazel or poplar. Flesh is solid, hard and brittle – it will break in pieces if dropped on a hard floor. Specimens can reach 12cm/5in in diameter and weigh 500g/1 lb, but most are around 30–50g/1–2oz. Season from late September, reaching best harvest time in November; provided the soil is not frozen, these truffles can be found until the end of January. A well-trained dog can detect the scent of a mature

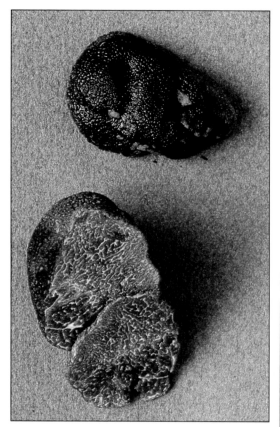

PERIGORD TRUFFLE, *TUBER MELANOSPORUM*

SUMMER TRUFFLE, *TUBER AESTIVUM*

*T. magnatum* 50 metres away, even if the truffle lies up to 50cm/20in underground. Attempts to grow *T. magnatum* commercially have failed.

### T. melanosporum

Famous are those of the Perigord region but this black truffle is also found in Provence and around Spoleto in Umbria and Norcia in Marche. It grows from mid November to March in symbiosis with oak: the roots of young trees are treated with spores before planting, ensuring a supply for commerce in these areas of France and Italy. The subterranean fruit-body is irregularly round, with rough black skin made up of hundreds of polygonal 'warts'. Flesh very solid, brittle, with a very pleasant smell, typically marbled brown with white veins which disappear on cooking, when the flesh turns black. Grows to maximum diameter of 7cm/2¾in and weighs 40–50g/1½–2oz (rare examples reach 100g/3½oz).

### T. aestivum

The 'summer' truffle usually grows between June and November, but has also been found through the winter, until March. Similar in appearance to *T. melanosporum*, but with skin covered in pyramidal black warts. Flesh a solid brown, with white veins which disappear on cooking, and a very delicate aroma. Round, to 3–4cm/about 1½in in diameter and 20–30g/about 1oz in weight. Found in England on chalk soils, usually favouring beech. Usually located not by trained dogs but by keen-eyed humans when a fraction of the warty skin of a truffle growing just below the surface is visible above ground. The luckiest person to have found large quantities of *T. aestivum* is without doubt Jenny Hall in Dover who has found some 150 examples of this tasty tuber in her own garden underneath an oak.

CLEANING AND COOKING

During the season you can often find me at my restaurant cleaning truffles, which I do with an almost religious reverence to avoid any waste. I never wash white truffles for fear of losing some of the aroma, but use one of those little brushes with brass bristles intended for cleaning suede. They can be used for cooking, but considering the high price I prefer to 'shave' them with a 'mandolino' raw over the food. When you buy them, make sure they are firm and heavy – and that any holes made by insects have not been filled with earth to make up the weight again, an important consideration when the price is £1 a gram!

White truffles are delicate and can be kept for a maximum of only 7 days after collecting. I suggest you buy a small quantity and use it straight away; in the restaurant where I need larger amounts, I keep them wrapped singly in tissue paper in a tightly closed plastic box in the refrigerator. Never leave any type of truffle in an open container in the refrigerator: the aroma will permeate all the other food around – unless, of course, you *want* everything to taste of truffles!

Black truffles keep much longer than white ones – up to 14 days when refrigerated. The tough warty skin has to be washed and scrubbed with a brush to dislodge earth. Edible raw, but usually used with cooked food.

If you have to transport a truffle at any time, Bput it in an airtight container with some raw rice to absorb moisture, but don't leave it for too long, or the truffle will deteriorate. When it becomes wet and soggy, it is of no further use and must be discarded.

No truffle takes kindly to being preserved. Freezing and drying are ineffective because the aroma is lost; bottling in water retains the texture but also allows most of the aroma to disappear. A paste of white truffles is now produced commercially in tubes and jars for using in sauces or for spreading on 'tartines'. One enterprising Italian company makes a natural essence of truffle, which I use for sauces and to flavour salad dressings. There is a very expensive olive oil with truffles which is also good for salads, but is mainly used to brush on meat before grilling.

# POISONOUS MUSHROOMS

Every year people from all walks of life and all over the world die as a result of eating poisonous mushrooms – victims of ignorance or of fallacies. No rule of thumb exists for telling whether a specimen is harmful or not: only accurate recognition and identification of individual mushrooms will tell you whether they are harmful or safe to eat, and, if safe, with what preparation.

One common fallacy is that if animals eat a mushroom without ill-effects, then it must be safe for humans. This is untrue: rabbits, for instance, which eat poisonous species with impunity, have entirely different digestive systems. The aroma gives no clue: *Armillaria mellea* smells quite pungent but (once cooked) is edible; *Amanita phalloides* (death cap), on the other hand, smells quite pleasant but is deadly poisonous. Some people think that if a mushroom turns blue when cut it is poisonous (others think the reverse), but both the poisonous *Boletus satanas* and the edible *Leccinum versipelle* share this characteristic. Other fallacies include such beliefs as that poisonous mushrooms turn parsley or garlic black, tarnish silver spoons and curdle milk, or that edible mushrooms growing near rusty iron or near known poisonous ones are themselves poisonous. You simply cannot tell from any such universal signs.

A mistaken belief is that all mushrooms lose their toxicity when dried or when cooked: the toxicity of the death cap is not affected by either process. On the other hand, certain mushrooms that are harmful when eaten raw become perfectly harmless when cooked. Others – some *Coprinus* species, for instance – have an adverse effect when taken with alcohol. You need to know the individual characteristics for each one – and then certain people turn out to be allergic or sensitive even to common mushrooms – as they might be to any kinds of food.

In between the 'edible and good' mushrooms at one extreme and the deadly poisonous ones at the other is a wide spectrum of more or less inedible ones. The 'poisonous' category includes both a few that are really deadly and a larger number that are indigestible and cause unpleasant stomach upsets of varying severity. In the 'rogues' gallery' portrayed here, I include both the deadly poisonous mushrooms that you need to know in order to avoid them completely, and a handful of 'look-alikes' with key ways of distinguishing them from their edible counterparts.

In the unfortunate event of your feeling unwell

after eating a suspect mushroom, seek immediate medical help and (if possible) take a sample of the mushroom with you so that the toxin may be identified.

FLY AGARIC, *AMANITA MUSCARIA*

YELLOW STAINER, *AGARICUS XANTHODERMUS*

FLY AGARIC, *AMANITA MUSCARIA*

## AGARICUS XANTHODERMUS

(syn PSALLIOTA XANTHODERMA)
Yellow Stainer

Superficially similar to *Agaricus arvensis* and *A. campestris*, the yellow stainer (as its name suggests) stains yellow immediately when cut or bruised, and smells rather inky. The field mushroom does not stain and smells pleasant and mushroomy; the horse mushroom may have a yellow tinge, but smells of aniseed.

Although not dangerously poisonous like *Amanita phalloides*, *Agaricus xanthodermus* can give you a painful and unpleasant time, with serious problems of respiration and digestion which manifest themselves in cold sweats and stomach pains soon after ingesting the mushrooms – but which can be remedied if quickly diagnosed and treated by a doctor. Strangely enough, some people are unaffected.

RECOGNITION

**Cap** spherical when young, becoming flat with age, to maximum diameter 15–16cm/6–6½in diameter; dirty white, becoming yellow when bruised or scraped. **Gills** pale pink at first, becoming brown with age. **Stem** white, staining chrome-yellow in bulbous stem base; 1–2cm/⅜–¾in diameter, to 15–16cm/6–6½in tall; with

pronounced white ring or skirt just below cap; often maggot-infested.

## AMANITA MUSCARIA

Fly Agaric

Perhaps the best-known poisonous mushroom, depicted by illustrators to conjure up the mysterious world of toadstools. There are stories about this mushroom all over the world, but the facts are that its toxins will attack the central nervous system producing such effects as intoxication, hallucination, euphoria, hyperactivity, coma and possibly death.

The only edible mushroom with which it could be confused is *Amanita caesarea* – the difference in mature specimens is clear, but the danger comes in trying to identify young specimens where the caps are just beginning to emerge from the egg-like volva from which all amanitas grow. In this situation, cut one in half lengthwise and check the colour of the gills and flesh: if these are white, then it is *Amanita muscaria*; if they are yellow, then it is *A. caesarea*.

RECOGNITION

Grows to maximum height of 25cm/10in including cap, which reaches 20cm/8in diameter.

DEATH CAP, *AMANITA PHALLOIDES*

**Stem** pure white, scruffy, with remains of volva attached to it, and white ring just below cap.
**Cap** bright red with scattered spots (the remains of the volva), but these can be washed off by rain leaving cap plain. In older specimens cap may fade to pale orange; there is a pale orange version in America. Grows from summer to autumn in mixed woodland, preferring birch and pine, and is extremely common. (Incidentally, when you see these beautiful mushrooms growing in the woods, survey the area carefully because some of the delicious boletus share the same habitat.)

## A. PHALLOIDES
Death Cap

Most of the fatal cases of mushroom poisoning that occur year after year all over the world can be attributed to this mushroom. It bears no resemblance to the edible mushrooms I have mentioned in this book (though it is similar to *Russula virescens* which is avidly sought by European collectors), but it is included here because it is all too easy for it to end up in your basket of edible mushrooms, put there in all innocence by a child anxious to help or by an unknowing adult. Even if you don't eat any it can cause illness, possibly serious, if its spores 'infect' your other mushrooms. If ever you find yourself in this situation, then throw them *all* away, including the edible ones. Wash your hands thoroughly after even touching it. This mushroom is so dangerous that you can afford to take no chances.

The trouble with *Amanita phalloides* poisoning is that despite years of research there is no simple antidote. In a simplified account, after ingestion the toxin passes through the digestive tract into the liver and kidneys, which it attacks; however, it is not passed out of the body with the other waste matter but is recirculated into the bloodstream to begin its journey all over again. Symptoms (severe diarrhoea and vomiting and stomach pains) start from 6 to 24 hours after ingestion, which is already too late: although the victim may appear to recover, death from kidney and liver failure shortly ensues.

The only consolation I can think of is that it is quite rare to find it in the mixed woodland where it grows from later summer to late autumn. Unless you are accompanied by an expert mycologist and want a specimen for studying gill structure and spores, I have to warn you – *do not touch it!*

RECOGNITION

Grows from egg-shaped volva which remains at the stem base. **Stem** quite tall, to 14cm/5½in and 1–2cm/⅜–¾in diameter, with white ring just under cap that becomes green with age. **Cap** to 12cm/5in diameter, round at first, becoming flattened; silky pale green to olive-green colour. **Gills** white, sometimes somewhat cream to pale green. *A. phalloides* var *alba* is entirely white and equally devastating.

## A. VIROSA
### Destroying Angel

The common name says a lot about this beautiful but lethal mushroom. I personally regard this as more dangerous than *A. phalloides* – not because it is more poisonous, but because, being all white in colour, it could be confused with some white edible mushrooms by a beginner. The poison is very similar to that of *A. phalloides* and it should equally be strictly avoided.

RECOGNITION

**Cap** white, to 12cm/5in diameter. **Gills** crowded

DESTROYING ANGEL, *AMANITA VIROSA*

and white (a distinguishing point between this and *Agaricus* species whose gills are pink, turning brown with age). **Stem** white, with fibrous surface and fragile indefinite ring; to 12cm/5in tall, and 1–1.5cm/⅜–½in diameter. In mixed or deciduous woods from late summer to autumn; not common.

## BOLETUS CALOPUS

This bolete is not poisonous in the lethal sense, but – like *Tylopilus felleus* – it is inedible due to its bitterness, which does not disappear on cooking. It can be mistaken for *Boletus luridus* and *B. erythropus* – but a good guidebook will help you identify these particular boletes.

RECOGNITION

**Cap** at first hemispherical, becoming flatter when mature; to 15cm/6in diameter. **Pores** yellowish, darkening with age; bruising bluish green. **Stem** the major identifying feature: to 10cm/4in tall and 5cm/2in diameter. Cylindric to slightly clavate, with a white network over a generally reddish or scarlet background, especially towards the base. Grows from late summer to late autumn, usually singly, in coniferous and broadleaved woodland.

*BOLETUS CALOPUS*

SATAN'S BOLETE, *BOLETUS SATANAS*

## BOLETUS SATANAS

Satan's Bolete

Fortunately this undesirable representative of the large family of delicious boletes is decidedly rare, and its distinguishing characteristics are so distinctive that there is little chance of making a mistake. Its appearance – especially when young, when it is very solid and bulbous – is similar to *Boletus barrowsii* or whiteking bolete, a form of *B. edulis* found in America growing under oaks.

*Boletus satanas* is said by some people to be edible after a long cooking process has destroyed the toxins, but what is the point of risking severe stomach upsets such as cramps, vomiting and diarrhoea when you can safely eat the other species? Generally I would advise you to leave alone any red-pored bolete you find which bruises blue.

RECOGNITION

**Cap** at first off-white, becoming grey or greenish grey; at first round, becoming flat and sometimes cracked with age; to 30cm/12in diameter. **Pores** very tightly packed, at first deep red becoming orange later, especially around the rim; turning bluish green when bruised. **Stem** enlarged below and onion-shaped; can reach 7–8cm/3in diameter even when young, sometimes being fatter than

the cap. Saffron-orange to bright lemon-yellow above, but red towards the base and with a red network, especially on the upper half. **Flesh** straw-colour in the cap, paler to whitish or lemon-yellow in the stem, changing to sky-blue. Grows beneath broadleaved trees such as beech and oak on calcareous soil from late summer through autumn; solitary, or in small groups of three or four.

## COPRINUS ATRAMENTARIUS

Common Ink Cap

Although it is edible when young, I am including this mushroom here because of its violent reaction when consumed with alcohol: nausea, palpitations and hot flushes not only can occur when beer, wine or liqueur is drunk at or just after the same meal, but to some extent are likely if alcohol is taken at the next meal, some hours later. Indeed, a chemical substance with properties similar to those contained in this mushroom is used to treat alcoholics.

It is a close relative of *Coprinus comatus* (shaggy ink cap), but the two are easy to distinguish.

RECOGNITION

**Cap** at first ovate, then conical when mature;

COMMON INK CAP, *COPRINUS ATRAMENTARIUS*

FALSE MOREL, *GYROMITRA ESCULENTA*

colour greyish, brownish towards the top, growing darker with age and blackening at margin when autodigestion takes place (as with *C. comatus*). **Gills** at first white, turning grey and then inky-black with autodigestion. **Stem** to 15cm/6in tall; thin (only 1–2cm/⅜–¾in diameter); hollow. Grows gregariously in tight clusters on stumps near cultivated areas, on lawns, in gardens and along roads, from late spring to late autumn.

## GYROMITRA ESCULENTA
### False Morel

The difference between this and the true morel is in the shape of the cap, which in *Gyromitra esculenta* consists of folded lobes and in *Morchella* species is made up of pits or hollows, and is usually more symmetrically shaped. As the epithet '*esculenta*' implies, some Europeans consider these mushrooms edible and regularly eat them after boiling them thoroughly or drying them, but cases of poisoning occasionally occur among apparently seasoned consumers. In the raw state these mushrooms are certainly very poisonous, so don't take chances and experiment.

RECOGNITION

To 12cm/5in high, sometimes irregular in shape. **Cap** made up of brain-like meandering folds and lobes, hollow; colour varying from pale tan to deep brown. **Stem** hollow; usually white; to 7cm/2¾in high and 2.4cm/1in diameter. Solitary or in small groups, usually under conifers but sometimes under hardwood, in spring.

## HYGROPHOROPSIS AURANTIACA
### False Chanterelle

This was originally classified as poisonous, was later declared edible, but recent findings tell us that ingestion of a large amount can cause digestive complaints. Beginners often mistake this common mushroom for the true chanterelle, *Cantharellus cibarius*.

RECOGNITION

**Cap** to 6cm/2½in diameter, varying from orange-yellow to darker orange in the centre. Margin at first inrolled, then flat. **Gills** concolorous with cap; decurrent, as in true chanterelle, but finer, and not extending so far down the stem. **Stem** less funnel-shaped than in true chanterelle;

FALSE CHANTERELLE, *HYGROPHOROPSIS AURANTIACA*

SULPHUR TUFT, *HYPHOLOMA FASCICULARE*

concolorous with cap or slightly darker; to 5cm/ 2in tall. **Flesh** not as substantial as in true chanterelle. Grows in late summer and autumn in mixed woodland, preferring conifers.

## HYPHOLOMA FASCICULARE

(syn NAEMATOLOMA FASCICULARE)
Sulphur Tuft

Sulphur tuft is an accurate description for both colour and manner of growth. This poisonous mushroom can cause symptoms that vary from a severe stomach upset to death; fortunately, its bitter taste is an additional deterrent to eating any quantities.

Though there are other differences, the simplest and surest way of ascertaining whether a cluster of mushrooms growing on an old stump is the excellent *Armillaria mellea* (honey fungus) or this poisonous mushroom is to look at the gills. In honey fungus these are white; in sulphur tuft they are a dull sulphur-yellow, becoming green with age. There are many more mushrooms that grow in clusters on wood, in similar conditions to those of sulphur tuft and honey fungus, and a good identification guide will describe the others in detail.

RECOGNITION

**Cap** to 8cm/3in when fully grown; yellow, with more orangey centre; sometimes having remains of veil attached to rim. **Gills** turn from yellow to green, and finally become dark purplish brown (the colour of the spores). **Stem** thin – 4–10mm/ ⅙–⅜ in diameter; varying from sulphur yellow when young to rusty brown when mature; with slight, insignificant ring zone on upper part of stem. Grows in clusters on old stumps, preferring decaying wood of deciduous trees, sometimes pine. Occasionally appearing to grow on soil, but in fact on buried stump or root. Very common; grows all year round, but most frequent in autumn.

## LACTARIUS TORMINOSUS

Woolly Milk Cap

Of the many *Lactarius* species, some are edible, many are inedible due to their taste, and some are distinctly poisonous. Mistakes are made between *Lactarius deliciosus*, which I like very much, and its poisonous counterpart *L. torminosus* – but it is easy to describe the key differences. There are parts of northern Europe and of Russia where this

WOOLLY MILK CAP, *LACTARIUS TORMINOSUS*

*OMPHALOTUS OLEARIUS*

mushroom is eaten after special treatment, but I recommend you to play it safe and leave it alone.

### RECOGNITION

Both mushrooms are similar in shape and size and both appear from summer to autumn. The most obvious difference is the woolly filaments covering the cap of *L. torminosus*. The cap can reach 12cm/5in diameter. The general cap colour is pinkish, and the gills and stem are flesh-coloured, whereas the overall tone of *L. deliciosus* is orange. A further difference is in the characteristic milk exuded from these mushrooms when they are cut: this is white in *L. torminosus* and saffron-red in *L. deliciosus*. *L. torminosus* grows mainly with birch, while *L. deliciosus* prefers conifers.

---

## OMPHALOTUS OLEARIUS

### (syn CLITOCYBE OLEARIA)

This poisonous lookalike of *Cantharellus cibarius* (the chanterelle) is fortunately rare in Britain (I have never seen it myself), and only occasional in central and southern Europe. In Mediterranean countries it generally grows on olive trees – hence the name *'olearius'* – though in America and Britain it grows on hardwood stumps. If in

springtime you visit a country where olive trees grow, don't get too excited by the sight of these mushrooms: they are not chanterelles – close inspection should show you the difference – and they should be left alone.

### RECOGNITION

The size of *Omphalotus olearius* is much greater than that of true chanterelles: it can reach 15cm/6in diameter. The cap colour is from dark orange to bright yellow – as in the chanterelle. The fact that it grows on trees is the final disqualifying factor in its comparison with chanterelles. Incidentally, this mushroom may be seen glowing in the dark – mature specimens have phosphorescent gills.

---

## SCLERODERMA CITRINUM

### (syn S. AURANTIACUM; S. VULGARE)
### Common Earthball

I am including this common mushroom so that you will not collect it thinking you have found a truffle or a puffball. Though it is not deadly poisonous, it can cause digestive problems and is best regarded as inedible.

Earthballs seem to grow everywhere, either solitarily or in small groups. When young they are

COMMON EARTHBALL, *SCLERODERMA CITRINUM*

BITTER BOLETE, *TYLOPILUS FELLEUS*

quite tempting – compact and fleshy. On maturity the flesh inside turns black – the colour of the spores, which are released when the outer skin or peridium cracks open. It is impossible to confuse them with *Langermannia gigantea* (giant puff-ball), which is pure white in colour and far greater in size than the 10cm/4in maximum which *Scleroderma citrinum* attains; species of *Lycoperdon* or small edible puffballs which are more similar in size tend to be pear- rather than globe-shaped. Confusion with truffles should be equally impossible, since truffles are hypogeal fungus – they grow underground, while earth-balls are epigeal and grow on the surface.

## TYLOPILUS FELLEUS

(syn BOLETUS FELLEUS)
Bitter Bolete

This bolete is not strictly poisonous, but as with *Boletus calopus* it is so terribly bitter that including a single specimen in a dish will spoil the whole thing. The possibility of mistaking it for *Boletus edulis* is more likely to occur in younger specimens, but if the mushroom is a little more mature, then the pink pores of *Tylopilus felleus* will distinguish it from *Boletus edulis*, which has

creamy-white pores. Both share the same habitat and appear from summer to late autumn.

RECOGNITION

**Cap** at first round, becoming flat later; light brown; to 12cm/5in diameter. **Pores** off-white in very young specimens, becoming pink with age and bruising brownish. **Stem** sturdy and fleshy – diameter to 3cm/1¼in at top and 6cm/2½in at base; to 12cm/5in tall. Net pattern on stem surface is another major identification point, particularly in comparison with *Boletus edulis*. *Tylopilus felleus* has a dark brown net pattern over a lighter background, while *Boletus edulis* has a white net pattern over a slightly darker background.

As a last resort, confirm your identification by tasting a little piece of the cap (and then spitting it out): if it is very bitter, then you have picked a specimen of *Tylopilus felleus* – and I'm afraid you will have to throw it away.

# GLOSSARY

*adnate* (of gills) see diagram

*adnexed* (of gills) see diagram

*ascomycetes* group of higher fungi whose spores are formed inside asci and released by pressure

*ascus (asci)* sac-like cell within which spores are formed

*basidiomycetes* major group of higher fungi including agarics etc whose spores are formed externally on club-shaped cells (basidia)

*bolete* mushroom with central stalk and tubes/pores rather than gills on the underside of the cap

*clavate* club-shaped

*cuticle* the 'skin' of the cap

*decurrent* (of gills) see diagram

*fibrillose* covered with small fibres

*frondose* broadleaved or deciduous (of trees)

*gasteromycetes* group of basidiomycetes where spores mature within the fruit-body, eg puffballs

*gills* blade-like strips of tissue that radiate on the underside of the cap eg in agarics

*gleba* spore-bearing fleshy tissue within gasteromycetes

*hymenium* spore-bearing fertile layer of asci, basidia etc

*hypha/-ae* minute individual filament from which mycelium and fruit-body are formed

*mycelium/-a* complex of hyphae: the vegetative portion of a fungus growing into the nutritive substrate/material

*mycorrhiza* symbiotic association of the mycelium with plant roots

*polypore* woody-textured fungus with tubes on underside of cap strongly attached to flesh

*pores* the mouths of the tubes in boletes and polypores

*reticulum* net-like mesh pattern on stalk of some boletes

*ring* remnant of a veil, present around stem of some agarics

*scabrous* rough granular or scaly texture on stem surface

*sessile* having no stem

*sinuate* (of gills) see diagram

*spore* the single reproductive unit of a fungus

*tubes* sponge-like spore-producing layer eg of boletes

*umbo* central swelling on cap of many agarics

*veil* protective membrane enclosing entire fruit-body (universal v.) eg in *Amanita* genus, or joining cap cuticle to stem (partial v.) eg in agarics

*volva* remains of universal veil forming cup-like sac around stem base eg in *Amanita*

# FURTHER INFORMATION

There is nothing like an expert to show the way safely. Information about local fungus forays is often available from public libraries and local natural history societies. Information can also be obtained from the following organizations – which, incidentally, welcome members of the public as associates:

**The British Mycological Society**
Maurice O. Moss PhD
(Membership Secretary)
Department of Microbiology
University of Surrey
Guildford, Surrey GU2 5XH

**North American Mycological Association**

# RECOMMENDED READING

Among the most useful reference books and field guides I would recommend:

Colin Dickinson and John Lucas *The Encyclopedia of Mushrooms* Orbis, 1979

Morton Lange & F. Bayard Hora *Collins Guide to Mushrooms and Toadstools* Collins, 2nd edition 1965

Roger Phillips *Mushrooms and Other Fungi of Great Britain and Europe* Pan Books, 1981

Derek Reed *Mushrooms and Toadstools* Kingfisher Ward Lock, 1980

David Arora *Mushrooms Demystified* Ten Speed Press, Berkeley, USA

# INDEX OF RECIPES

# INDEX OF MUSHROOMS

Page numbers in **bold type** indicate a full description in the Field Guide. Numbers preceded by R: are the recipe references relevant to that mushroom. An asterisk (*) indicates a poisonous or inedible species.

## ACKNOWLEDGEMENTS

My special thanks to the following people who have contributed in one way or another to my love of nature and in particular to my love of fungi:

Servilia Alzetta, Bobby Baker, Albino Barberis, Flo Bayley, Peter Bazalgette, the Bolzoni and Carluccio families, Christina Borkowska, David Brittain, Piero Cerruti, Gennaro Contaldo, Santiago Cortes, Phil Cutler, Penny David, Clive Frost/British ELLE/Transworld for photographs, Irina Holt, Julio Gallo, Giovanni Gizzi, Judith Hahn, Jenny and John Hall, Bernard Higton, Christina Ivel, Stan Jaworsky, Elsbeth Juda, Dr Kaversky, Raymond Lawince, Angelo Letini, Jay Madow, Stanley Marcus, Sandro Maldini, Dr Carlo Meluccio, Sarah Metzner, Sarah Miller, Jeremy Mills, Susan Mitchell, Paola Navone, Sir Sidney Nolan, Eduardo Paolozzi, Lucy and Granby Patrick, Raul from Portugal, Dr Derek Reed, Ruggero Ruggeri, Dora Santarlasci, Zimmie Sasson, Frank Spolnik, Vicky Stangroom, Barbara Swiderska, Paul Tapelor, David Thomas, Colin Webb, Ann Willitts, Andrew Whittuck, John Woodcock for line drawings, Gillian Young, Inge Zerunian, all journalists who have written articles on fungi, and The Conran Shop for props used in the studio photography.

I hope that we can all enjoy the gentle world of mycology for many years to come. This book is for everyone who shares my dread of the deadliest mushroom of all – the one in the form of a cloud.